Crosses to Bear
Love to Share

A Dedication to Single Mothers

Published by Six Hearts Publishing

Six Hearts
publishing

Library of Congress Control Number: 93-093636
First Edition August 1997, Second Edition, June 2010
ISBN: 0-9845767-0-3

Cover design © 2010 David A. Campbell
Text pages design, Huntley Burgher
Photographer/Author, back cover: Don Parchment

Published by Six Hearts Publishing
Some names and identifying details have been changed to protect the identities of the individuals involved.

For your publication needs visit: www.sixheartspublishing.com
Six Hearts Publishing is a registered trademark of Six Hearts Inc

IC 041. US 100 101 107. G & S: book publishing, newspaper publishing, magazine publishing, publishing of reviews, publishing of electronic publications.

Dedication

This book is dedicated to all single mothers & their most valued investments.... their children

Acknowledgements

But for the grace of God, I could have been a patient in a mental institution. I am grateful to God for preserving mine and my children's lives, despite the pain we've endured. I do believe everything happens for a reason, Genesis 50 verse 20, says it best: "You intended to harm me, but God intended it for good, to accomplish what is now being done, the saving of many people." (NIV). At this phase of my life there is no hatred in my heart towards anyone, I have forgiven everyone who might have caused me grief, because the experience has left me with a burning desire to help others, especially single mothers.

My sincerest gratitude to all my family and friends who've stood by me over the years. Special thanks to Dr. Garth Rose who worked with me on the original version and provided input on the revised edition. To my six children who have loved me unconditionally, Jason, Leighton, Leneen, David, Paul and Trish-Ann I'll love you forever.

CHAPTER ONE

I am convinced that one of the most beautiful and serene places in the entire world is rural Jamaica, the pearl of the Caribbean. The good Lord placed a kiss on this earth, when he made it, and decreed the island Jamaica, the land of flora and fauna. This is my land, the land of my birth. A land made even more beautiful by a kaleidoscope of colors. The scenic blue waters and green hills, exotic trees and brilliant golden sunshine are all the necessary ingredients for an island of paradise.

Agatha Harding is in her ninth month of pregnancy and is expecting her eleventh child. Her husband, Valentine Harding, is a man who is loved by the people of the district, and cherished by his wife.

Agatha, seated in the living room, hears Valentine approaching. As he entered the living room he could hear her moans faintly. Her suffering and his hopelessness brought tears to his eyes. He placed his hands gently on her forehead.

"Honey, you seem very weak but thank God you're conscious."

With a heavy heart Val stepped away and stood staring through the dark as he watched the rain drops hammering against the windows. Again, he moved towards her and laid his hand lightly on her head and prayed.
"Dear God, please give her strength and keep her with me."

His wife turned her pain racked face to him and quietly whispered.

"Dear, I don't think I'm going to make it this time."

The Doctor warned Val that at the onset of labor he should waste no time in getting his wife to the hospital, which was approximately thirty five miles away. He was concerned that if she attempted to have the child at home, as she did the other ten, her chances of survival would be slim. It was a miracle that she survived until this point. His frustration deepened when he realized that there was a strong possibility that the roads might be blocked because of the rains. If that was the case, they could be trapped in the district for as long as a week, or for that matter, for as long as it took to clear the roads. There was no time to waste and in less than an hour he had his wife appropriately dressed for the weather. He carried her gently and placed her on the back seat of the car. Then he carefully drove through the storm.

By the time they arrived at the hospital Agatha's pains were unbearable. She was immediately admitted and rushed to the delivery room. Val nervously paced the floor of the lobby all night. The following morning, August 19th, was a beautiful day. Val stood by a window of the waiting room filled with anticipation when suddenly a nurse approached him.

"Good morning Mr. Harding, I have good news. Your wife just gave birth to a beautiful baby girl! Please follow me."

Valentine followed her to the nursery. He looked through the viewing glass and saw his daughter, seven pounds eight ounces, with jet black hair and a tiny pink face. He was moved to tears but thankful for the safe delivery of the baby.

As soon as he was satisfied that his wife was in stable condition he rushed back to the country to visit his aunt Nora, who was dying. He wanted desperately to inform her of the baby's birth before she passed.

When Aunt Nora heard the news, she was visibly happy, despite her critical condition. She was already losing her speech, so Valentine found it difficult to understand what she was trying to say. After several attempts, he finally understood.

"Call the baby Nora."

She struggled as she conveyed this message. Valentine smiled, squeezed her hand and assured her that her wishes would be granted. Those were her parting words. Though saddened by his Aunt's death, he was consoled that his baby girl would be carrying the name of someone who was very special to him. She had been a woman of strength, God fearing, loving, kind and understanding. One who took time to listen to the cries of the people, and one to whom many regarded as their role model.

I, Nora Harding, was born a fighter. From a fetus in the womb I fought to survive, despite my mother's illnesses. As I grew and the pattern of my life was shaped, I was determined, with the grace of God, to overcome every obstacle.

Christianity was an important part of my upbringing. My parents were not just preachers of Christian love but doers. This was their life and they made a great effort to impart this teaching to us. Papa was very caring and a humorous person. He genuinely loved Mama and their wedding vows were sacred. They had the normal marital differences but they were always discussed in private. They lived by the precept, 'Never let the sun go down on your wrath.' Papa also believed that in accordance with the scriptures, a husband should love his wife just as how Christ loved the Church. It was with this strong commitment that he entered into, and shared a lasting relationship with Mama.

He was the breadwinner and an excellent provider. He did not feel threatened or humiliated by Mama, who had to supplement the family's income in the later years when the grocery business took a turn for the worse. We needed divine intervention as only a miracle could save the business. The creditors served them an ultimatum; pay the debts or lose the business. All seemed lost, but my mother would not accept this.

She was determined to put her faith to the test. She fasted and prayed day and night for a miracle. The day before the creditors were to come and close down the whole operation, a wealthy man who resided in England drove up to the country. Without any prompting, inquired of my parents about purchasing fifty acres of their land. As if in direct answer to Mama's prayer, the amount the man offered was sufficient to pay the creditors. This was indeed a miracle, and my parents immediately entered into the agreement and were able to settle their debt. Unfortunately, the decision was made to shut down the bakery but the grocery store remained open.

Closing the bakery was heart breaking, especially for Papa. One day the family sat under a large apple tree in our yard and reflected. Papa seemed especially sad.

Because of the loss of income, right around that time my eldest brother Lenworth approached my parents and asked if I could leave home and live with him and his wife, they agreed.

I was only eight years old at the time but was willing to do whatever it took to improve the financial situation at home. Lenworth and I had developed a very close relationship which made his wife Cheryl jealous at times.

I found my sister-in-law to be abusive as she often beat me for things that even Mama would have overlooked. Being afraid of my new surroundings and an abusive guardian, I often wet the bed. One morning after waking up from a series of nightmares not only were my panties wet but the sheets and mattress were soaked.

I knew I was going to pay for it but was not ready to face the challenge so early in the morning. I made a big pile to cover up my sin and hurried off to school. That day I prayed for sickness so I would end up in the hospital and not have to go home. I didn't become ill so as I walked thru my doors I was grabbed by my sister-in-law beating me with a leather belt as she spoke.
"What are you doing wetting my damn bed? You should be ashamed of yourself a big girl like you and still pissing bed. I promise when I'm done with you today you'll want to go back to your mother."

Behind the house was a large pigsty, with a few dozen pigs. With my behind very sore, from the beating, and my eyes almost blinded with tears, I found myself being pushed in the pigs' pen by my sister-in-law Cheryl. She locked the gate and as she walked away she said.

"I'd rather you sleep with the pigs than wet my damn bed!"

'Is this for real or am I still having the nightmares?' I thought to myself.

When I felt the pigs biting at my feet, it jarred me to my senses and I knew it wasn't a dream.

'How could God allow this to happen to me?' I questioned.

At that moment I decided to return home to my parents and escape this evil woman. Even though I loved my brother, he was an adult and had to bear his crosses alone. After two hours of torture she released me. By then my hatred for her was overpowering and I prayed that God would remove me from her. Although I returned home, that experience threatened to play havoc with my self-esteem.

The financial situation had worsened at home and the decision was made for Mama to seek employment in the United States. This was a tough decision for Papa but with the assistance of a helper he was willing to take on the challenge.

We intimidated the poor soul as she could not measure up to our mother's standards. She could not cook, so a lot of the food was fed to the dogs.

Kevin, the youngest brother, prepared our meals and to our surprise, they were even better than Mama's. Papa enjoyed good food, and thought Kevin had tapped into a God given talent. Mama returned to Jamaica around the time I graduated from high school. Though I was happy to see Mama, I was extremely busy with planning the graduation as I was the president of the graduating committee.

CHAPTER TWO

With only a week away, the fifth formers got together, and planned a picnic to one of Jamaica's most beautiful spots, Duns River Falls in Ocho Rios. It was an enjoyable day. We swam, climbed the famous falls, and played ball. While playing on the beach I felt as though I was being watched. Following my intuition, I turned around, and there, sitting under one of the beach huts, was quite an interesting character. He sat alone, wearing a faded blue shirt with jeans, and a pair of dark glasses. His presence was so strong, that he unnerved me. When the game was finished, I sat on the sand totally exhausted.

The stranger walked up to me, "So you are Miss Harding? I have heard so much about you. I understand that you are responsible for planning the graduation ball. Well, I just want to let you know, that I'll be taking you."

I looked up at him in utter shock, telling myself that I couldn't have heard right. 'This man must be out of his mind,' I thought.

Then I replied, "Listen, I don't know you, and with your attitude, I don't care to. You're taking me to the ball?" I said sarcastically. Do you think you're God's gift to women and I should consider myself lucky? For your information, there are six young men waiting for an answer from me, and I don't recall you being one of them. It just doesn't work like that."
He paused and then replied, "You can say whatever you want, but this is not a coincidence, its destiny. I came here to meet with you today, and here we are. Together!"

The presumptuousness of the man shocked me, but despite his brashness, I had an admiration for him. Graduation was only one week away, so he had very little time to convince me. Feeling somewhat curious, I relaxed and decided to chat with him for a while.

"By the way my name is Larry Bell, and I'm still trying to figure out why we didn't meet in school. As a matter of fact, I left school the same year you started, so close, and yet so far. But it's not too late to make up for all the lost time. You might not believe this, but prior to today, I made some inquiries about you. I found out that you are Miss Popularity, the queen of St. Helen's.
Am I not right?"

I didn't answer, so he continued, "Well I have introduced myself and it would be common courtesy for you to do likewise."

I made an effort to be cordial, and extending my hand, I said, "Hi Larry, I'm Nora Harding, and I'm very pleased to meet you."

He held onto my hands, and looking into my eyes, he spoke with conviction, "Nora, it is indeed a pleasure to meet you, and mark my word, this will be the most memorable day of your life."

I could not believe my ears! This man had so much charisma.

'Was this good luck or what?'

I really wasn't sure what it was, but he seemed to have some sort of hold on me. As he spoke, I tried to figure out whether or not I knew anything about him, maybe from the other guys in school, but I couldn't remember anything except his name. I wondered who could fill me in on this guy. I had to satisfy my curiosity, but didn't know where to start. He sensed that I was deep in thought, and interrupted.
"A glass of ice soda wouldn't hurt?"

"That sounds good," I replied.

He jumped to his feet and walked off, kicking the sand, hands in pocket, staring at the ground. I looked up at his medium frame, about 5'10"tall, a good-looking man, with dark complexion. I found him mysterious. There was something different about him, but I couldn't figure out what it was. I was in a state of confusion.

"So Miss Harding…"

"Stop, Larry please call me Nora, Miss Harding sounds a bit too formal."

He hands me an ice cold glass of soda.

"Thanks, this will certainly help."

"Nora, you have a unique way of expressing your affection. Interesting!" He seemed excited.

"What exactly are you talking about?" I asked.

"Nora, when I decided to investigate you, I must admit that I was captivated with the feed-back. One person in particular commented,

'Oh, she, she's a nice person, but undoubtedly, she's a flirt.' What do you have to say about that Miss Harding?"

I did not respond. For a minute, I felt like walking away from his little mind games, but I thought it was important to clear up his misconception of me.

"Let me explain something here. I cannot help being liked by guys. It is true that I'm very popular in school. But let me set the record straight once and for all. Although most of my friends are men, I am not in a committed relationship. They have made several attempts to become sexually involved with me, but I can hold my head high, knowing that not one of them can point a finger at me. To this day, I remain untouched. Since you seem so interested, I will confess, that the most I have done is kiss a couple of guys, but that's about it."

With a look of relief he said, "So are you trying to tell me that you're still a virgin?"

I felt as though I was being interrogated, all these questions.

"Larry, quite frankly I wasn't really trying to tell you anything, but yes, I am a virgin, now, does that put your mind at ease?"

He could not conceal the sly grin.

"Mmmmm, something to think about. How about us getting out of the sun and go spend some time in the water? At least that will cool us down."

"In a second, but I'd rather climb the falls instead." I replied.
"I'll be delighted to accompany you, come on, let's go."
He hurriedly pulled off his jeans, under which he was wearing his trunks and

extending his hand, he pulled me to my feet.

As we began climbing the falls, I observed that one of the girls from our group who was a senior, was slightly annoyed seeing me with Larry. As we passed her, she tossed a pebble towards me, which hit me on my ankle. I was very offended, and decided that if she was trying to get Larry's attention she would have to try doubly hard, because I was not about to let up. One way or another I had to get back at her. All during this, Larry's ego was being fed, and the message was subtle.

'Here is this girl, dying for me to give her a little attention, yet you've got it all, and you seem to be taking it for granted?'

I had an interest to hear more about him so he started out by telling his life's story.

"Nora, I've been in the military for the past two years, the last ten months, I spent in Sand Hurst, England, where I was involved in an intensive officer's training course. My plans were to stay there and graduate as a lieutenant, but this didn't happen. I was involved in a dangerous racial incident, which resulted in my being expelled from the army. Now here I am, living at my father's place and just chillin' for the time being."

He stood still, appearing as though he had a divine revelation, and in a prophetic tone he uttered.

"So this is in fact, a blessing in disguise! If this had not happened, chances are, we'd have never met…"

I was more interested in what led to his expulsion from the military.
"So what was the incident that brought about your dismissal?" I asked.

"I was anticipating that question. I'm not trying to be evasive, but it's difficult for me to discuss it. You might not be able to relate to this, but I go through severe mental changes whenever the issue comes up. So please don't ask me to go through that right now, it would definitely change the tone."

"No problem Larry, whatever you say. Would it be alright to ask, if you have any plans in finding a job?"

"Nora, you're free to ask anything, but with all that I've been through, I need a long cooling out period and finding a job is certainly not a priority right now."

"So how do you plan to get money to live? Can your father afford to support you?"

"He's not been complaining, and why are you asking all these questions anyway?"

"I'm trying to get to know you. Is something wrong with that?"

He remained silent, and I was becoming annoyed. I paused for a moment then continued, "In my opinion, you, as an adult, should make every effort to provide for yourself and not rely on anyone else to do so. I'm sure your father has done his part. Don't you think you should be taking care of him instead?"

He was not amused, and I could tell from his response.

"Why are you so concerned? What you don't understand is that my father owes this to me. You're not even armed with all the facts. But to address your concerns, my father is well set, he's a big inspector at his job and he makes decent money. He has two homes down here and acres and acres of land. He understands what I've been through, and knows that it will take some time for me to get over it, unlike you. But on a more serious note, if you want us to remain friends, just don't try finding me a job. I will do that when I'm ready."

As I glanced at his facial expression, I knew he was trying hard to conceal the anger. I sensed that the timing was not right for me to be exposed to it, so I backed off. All along we were holding hands, then suddenly, he let go of my hand and went ahead, hastily rushing to the bottom of the falls, where we had started out.

By the time I joined him, he once again displayed a charming, caring personality, almost leaving doubts in my mind about his expressions of anger only a moment ago. I tried to relax and adjust to his warm temperament. It was then that we noticed, that the majority of the group had left, and only a handful of us remained. We made our way to the main road where we tried to hitch a ride, but we had no luck. As time passed we were laughing and talking, when I saw my brother Clifford driving toward us in one of his trucks.

I shouted to the others, "Hey guys, get ready to hop in, our ride is here."

"Nora how do you know he will give us a ride?" Larry asked.
"I don't think he could explain to Mama and Papa the reason why he left his sister on the street."

Clifford called out to us as he pulled over to the side of the road.
"I guess you guys knew I was coming so you were waiting on me, right? Some of you lovely ladies can sit up front with me, and the guys can hop in the back."

Of course, driving home with Clifford had a big disadvantage. My evening ended abruptly as everyone was dropped off at the school, and me, I had to take a seat next to him, as he drove me home. All through the night my thoughts were obsessed with my rendezvous that day.

The following morning I packed a few items of clothing, as my friend April had extended an invitation to spend the weekend at her house. She was having a pre-graduation party, so most of the guests were from school. April's house was a lovely one, located on a hill overlooking the ocean. I was surprised when I learned that Larry only lived within walking distance of April's house. His father's house was situated at the foot of the hill. Prior to Larry's meeting me, she had extended a neighborly invitation to him to attend the party, so I knew he would be there.

The night of the party I was busy, assisting in serving the guests as they poured in. Feeling anxious, I glanced around the room a few times to see if Larry arrived, but I didn't see him. I stopped serving the drinks and responded to an invitation to dance with one of the guys from school. While we danced, I felt a tap on my shoulder.

"Nora, I'll be waiting outside when you're through."
Mac, my dance partner, looked at me, taken-aback.

"Nora are you dating Larry?"
"Not really, I just met him, and there seems to be a mutual attraction, but that's basically it, nothing concrete."

"Nora, you know I've always liked you, but right now I have no axe to grind because I'm going out with April, but I really don't think that guy is your type. He's crazy! I'd hate to see you hurt. Anyway remember he's waiting for you, and he's not the kind of guy you keep waiting. He'll come in and start a fight and crash the party before you know it."

"I'm afraid I can't agree with you Mac, that's not what I'm seeing."
I left and went outside to meet Larry. As I walked up to him he asked,
"Did you dress up this pretty for Mac?"

"What are you talking about? Mac and April are going steady, he's my friend and

that's it. Take it or leave it."
"Just kidding, thought I'd pull your legs a little bit."
I thought to myself, 'Was he really pulling my legs or was he jealous?'

"Do you feel like dancing or would you rather stay out here and talk for a while?"
He asked.

"Larry, I'm cool. It's up to you this time."

"Okay, let's dance," he said. The D.J. was playing a slow song.

He held me very close as he sung every word in my ear. After dancing for approximately thirty five minutes, we both became a little uncomfortable as it was very warm inside.

"Let's take a stroll Nora and view the awesome scenery, and enjoy this beautiful moonlit night."

He took me by the hand as he led me through the crowd, away from the party.

"Nora, I would love to take you out on my father's boat tonight."

"That would be nice Larry, let's do it."

"I'm sorry, we can't. If only I had thought about it earlier, I would have gotten the keys, but Dad is sleeping and I'm not about to wake him."

 I believed him, as he was as serious as one could ever be.
"Well, if we can't go out on the boat tonight, I guess we can do it some other time," he said.

We spoke about my childhood. So I told him how I was raised and a little about my parents and how committed they were to God and each other. He appeared sad.

"Did I say something wrong?" I asked.

"Nora you haven't said anything wrong. I only wish that I could have been surrounded with as much love as you were. Maybe God has really brought you into my life for a special reason, to teach me how to love. Nora, I need you. There's a big void in my life that needs to be filled, and coming from a broken home and trying to fend for myself at an early age, I never had the opportunity to understand the true meaning of love.

My previous girlfriend left me for another man, but made me believe all along that I was the only one in her life. My mother left me at an early age, taking all my sisters, leaving me with my father, who has a severe drinking problem.

I enrolled in the military, thinking that it would make me forget my past and help me look forward to a brighter future, but again, another disappointment. I wasn't given the chance to complete the course. I'm at a crossroad in my life, and you are all I need to make my life complete. I want you to be mine. I really do need you."

As I listened, I tried to think of ways to reach out and touch him and let him know that someone really cared.

'Do I have to love him? Or, must I fall in love with him in order to reach him?

I knew I had to start somewhere, and I made a commitment to start by loving him that night. I reflected on how I felt the time when my sister-in-law shoved me in the pigs sty, and how I wished that someone would have been there to reassure me that I was loved.'

We spent the greater portion of that night together. The following day was hectic, as it was the big day we'd all been waiting for.

'Graduation day was finally here!'

When Larry picked me up, he was flabbergasted.

"The lady of the night, Nora you look stunning,"

"Thank you Larry, you're looking very sharp too."

When he drove into the schoolyard, he could not believe his eyes. The girls in the graduating class were all dressed in red and white evening gowns. Everything looked magnificent. Kevin had outdone himself and the auditorium and décor reflected his God given talent.

"Man oh man, is your brother really responsible for this?" Larry asked.

"I'm impressed. What other talents do you guys have in your family?"

I experienced a keen sense of accomplishment. This was the very first event

for Kevin since he graduated from culinary arts school. I went over to him and introduced him to Larry. Then I leaned over, and whispered.
"Kevin I'm very proud of you, I couldn't have made a better decision than having you cater the event."

In turn he hugged me, "Nora I love you, and don't worry we're going to be doing some big things in the future."

Musical entertainment was provided by one of Jamaica's leading bands, The Fantastic Five. As the music played and the lovely rhythms floated through the air, I took note of the various expressions of the guests throughout the auditorium. Everyone was enjoying themselves as I overheard some of the comments.

"Who's really responsible for this event?"
"How come this has never been done before?"
"Where did the money come from to put on this type of function?"
I remained quietly amused, hoping that all would go well.

Intent on seeing that everything was under control, I left Larry for a while. On returning, I was amazed to see him making a pass at one of the girls who I knew to have had a crush on him. I was annoyed and remarked.

"Am I interrupting something?"

As I attempted to walk away Larry turned to me saying.
"Nora, I'm sorry, I was just passing the time until you got back."
I turned around and looked at the girl who was pleasantly amused. Walking side by side with me he kept saying how sorry he was.

"Listen Larry, why don't you go back and finish what you started, so I can get on with the night?"

"Nora, you don't understand. Can you please step outside with me so we can discuss this? Please!"
As I followed him outside, seeds of doubts were sown in my mind.
'Do I really need this? Here is this man head over heels crazy about me, and almost in front of my face trying to kiss this other girl. This might be more trouble than I care to handle.'
Then I remembered my commitment to love him and teach him love, I felt like a missionary more than anything, and I couldn't turn back now."

After his plea, I was even more willing to forgive him. After all, he was far more advanced in life's experiences than I was. He was five years my senior and had been out in the real world, experiencing hardships, pain, joy, sorrow. He had been under the regimentation of the military, and had almost made it to the upper echelons. I was enthralled by his achievements. Yet, it never occurred to me that we might not be compatible.

CHAPTER THREE

It was a cool, sunny Wednesday afternoon, about six weeks since I had met Larry, during this time we had been spending a lot of time together. This day, there was a big fair in Town so we both went. We were so much in love, or maybe it was lust, but we were kissing passionately in the open, not caring how other folks felt or what they'd say. Up to this point, he had made several attempts to make love to me, but I was too afraid to try.

While at the fair, we went on the rides together, we danced and ate, and the only thing that was left for us to do, was to go some place private, and once and for all, give in to our desires. Things started to move very fast, and we were like two dogs in heat, seeking to find somewhere to lay. His father's house was the most likely place to go, as it was not too far away. We left the fair without any specific plan, as I was just going along with the flow.

When we arrived there, the place was cold and desolate it didn't feel like a home at all. I wondered if 'love' had ever visited this dwelling. There was a crisp, dry breeze blowing through the windows, it brought no affection, it brought no warmth, it brought no love. This atmosphere did nothing for my already deflated emotions, and I thought we'd have been better off, if we'd stayed at the fair.

My passion and expectations died immediately and I became cold and isolated like the house itself. Larry, on the other hand, seemed totally unaffected by the surrounding. I tried to relax and decided to look to him for guidance. He was the pro, I was the amateur, so I was willing to learn. When he took off his pants, the reality of the moment hit me and I felt ashamed. I buried my head in the pillow and refused to look up.

"Nora it's alright, we're not doing anything wrong, just try to relax and you'll be enjoying this in no time."

I barely raised my head, and timidly replied, "Larry, you don't understand. If my mother ever knew where I was and what I was doing she'd disown me. I know this is wrong, and sooner or later, I'm going to have to pay. It just doesn't seem right Larry. Let's forget it for now and at least wait until we get married."

"Are you for real? You must be the only virgin at eighteen, so don't worry, the key is to relax."

By this time I'm sitting up in the bed with my legs crossed and the pillow in my lap, using it as a security blanket.

"Larry what is to say that if I have sex with you now, we're going to end up getting married?" He cleared his throat conveniently.

"Well I can't talk for you, but as for me, I have never felt this way about anyone before, so we can get married as soon as you like."

"Larry, don't be silly, it's not as easy as that. I'm talking about, over a period of time. But do you think we'll end up getting married?"

"Come on Nora, tell me, why wouldn't we? There is absolutely no doubt in my mind."

"Larry, I was brought up to believe that a woman only gets intimately involved with her husband and if I'm going to risk it now, somewhere down the road we'll have to end up together. I preserved my body for my husband, and Larry what if it's not you?"

"Baby, you want it to be me, then it will be me, so just relax…please….just for me Nora, please relax."

"Okay, Larry, Okay, start then!" He pulls down my panties.
"Dear God,"I whispered."Please don't' strike me dead like the people of Sodom and Gomorrah."

He could tell from my actions that I was petrified, and felt guilty.
"Nora, are you okay?" I didn't know if everything was alright as I didn't know what to expect.

"I guess I am, but am I supposed to feel anything?"

Hearing Larry's groans, I thought he was in pain.
"Larry, are you alright?"I asked.
"I guess not, I don't know if it's my past or what, but nothing seems to be happening."

"So are you almost finished then?"
Sounding surprised at my question, he replied,
"Nora I've not even started yet."
"Oh, you've not, I didn't realize. When will I know?"

"As soon as my mind is settled, trust me, you'll know the difference."
Two or three hours maybe, but it was a long time to wait, and then it finally happened.

'Is this what I was waiting for?'I wondered.
Based on what I was told by my girlfriends. I should have heard musical instruments and see stars floating in the twilight zone. However I didn't hear or see anything, the only thing I can recollect was Larry saying.

"Nora, thank you for being so understanding."

Although a little disappointed, all psychological blocks were removed and our ties became stronger. Shortly after we consummated our relationship, I had to leave the rural area to live with Kevin and my older sister Vanessa in the city. It was mandatory at that time to serve the Government in a National Youth Service program for one year. I was assigned to a Salvation Army prep school, where I was trained in helping to develop the academic skills of young children. I thoroughly enjoyed working with them. They were innocent and easily influenced. I made a concerted effort to make a positive contribution to their lives.

My favorite student was Julius Mahfood, a handsome little boy, who was unusually intelligent for his age. Often times I'd hope to have a son like Julius. This training was really preparing me for teacher's college, as I felt a sense of obligation in fulfilling my father's dream.

One evening when Larry came to visit we sat quietly on the front porch, enjoying the cool evening breeze. A good thirty minutes passed before he broke the silence.

"Nora do you think you could spend the rest of your life with me?"
I was hesitant to answer as he caught me off guard, I thought for a minute then replied,"I don't see why not. Yes I will."

"Nora, I must marry you. Never in my life has anyone taken the time to treat me the way you have. You've won my heart and please take it, it's all yours. All I can do Nora, is commit myself to loving you, and you only. I will not share my life with any other, and always remember, 'my word is my bond.'

"Larry I believe you, and all my love is yours too, so you have nothing to worry about."

Having the privacy of the house to ourselves he had my undivided attention. I served him a delicious meal, mouth watering desert and my young flawless body. We ended up under my powdered sheets giving our souls and our love to each other.

CHAPTER FOUR

A few weekends went by, and Princess, a friend of mine from high school was celebrating her 18th birthday, and invited myself and Larry to the party. The majority of the crowd consisted of students from my graduating class. Larry stuck to me like glue, and I found it strange that most of the guys were very distant, while some of the girls pretended as though they didn't know me. This concerned me, as I had a great rapport with my peers, and was known for my sociable behavior. Despite the large and familiar crowd, I felt confined being with Larry.

We were talking outside when he stepped away to get us some drinks. While he was gone Princess's fourteen year old brother, Adrian, came up to me, telling me how pretty I looked. He was more like a younger brother, so I regarded his comments as a compliment. His eyes caught the diamond cross pendant that Mama had given me,"Gee Nora, that's so beautiful."
He took the pendant in his hands admiring it,"Where did you get this?"

As he admired the pendant Larry walked up. Before I even had a chance to answer him, Larry rudely interrupted,"Nora, I must speak with you. NOW!"
Astonished by the tone of his voice and his stern look, I followed him to a far corner of the lawn, away from the party. He stopped sharply, then swung around facing me.

"Look I know that damn little boy is trying a thing with you, and it is very obvious that you are encouraging him. I was just in time to see him removing his hand from your breast, and you did nothing to stop him. I will kill him, I will kill his ass, because I don't want anyone messing with my woman. But on the other hand, what type of woman are you, to allow this little boy to step out of line and you stand there enjoying it? This is not saying much for you. Do me a favor, and tell Adrian to stay away from you, or I will mess him up for good. I refuse to be played for a damn fool again. As for you, you'll never get the opportunity to two-time me, I'd kill your ass before I let that happen."

I was scared stiff.'What was this all about?' I wondered.
I was at a loss for words; I was so frightened that I began to cry. I had no interest in returning to the party. All I wanted was to escape, get away from everyone, bury my face somewhere and hide.

I followed him to his car and leaned on the front door, he came over, opened the door and I slowly sank in the seat. I still didn't understand what had happened. As we drove away from the party neither of us said a word. About a mile and a half later he broke the silence.

"Nora, I'm sorry. Okay?"

I said nothing.

"Do you understand that you're all I've got, and I'd rather die than lose you? Please accept my apology. This will be the first and the last time that you'll ever experience anything like this. I simply lost control. What transpired tonight was never intended for you, but it's unfortunate, that I end up hurting the person who means the most to me. Nora, I'm truly sorry. If you didn't mean anything to me, I'd just leave the party and walk away from everything, but not from you Nora, I refuse to do that with you. I know men don't like to admit this, but I'm so jealous of you. I didn't mean to hurt or disrespect you, but as God is my witness, this type of behavior will never ever be repeated."

I believed every word he said, and by the time he was through, I felt sorry for not being more understanding of his feelings. I was convinced that his violent action was a spill over from the incident in the army, his lonely upbringing and his heart broken relationship.
'What emotional turmoil?'I thought.

Yes, I was prepared to assist in the healing process but I didn't communicate this as I felt such pity for him. Instead, I made him feel that I was contemplating ending the relationship. When he dropped me home that night I remained quiet and saddened, leaving him with a feeling of uncertainty. I deliberately avoided contact with Vanessa and Kevin as I had to conceal'the other side'of Larry.

The next morning I kept thinking about Larry's shocking outburst when Kevin knocked lightly on my door. I was not in the mood to talk but he came in and was observing me for a while. Suddenly I became nauseous and tried hard to disguise it. I didn't want to think of what the possibility could be. So walking towards the door Kevin sarcastically said, "I suggest you go to the doctor, because I'm almost sure you're pregnant."

For that moment I didn't like Kevin at all because he was not being nice to me.

"Kevin, I'm sure that I'm not pregnant. But, I've been wanting to say something to you. I know that you don't like Larry, but I'm not him, so why do you have to be so indifferent towards me?"

"Nora, I'm not about to argue with you, here's some money, take it, call a cab and go see the doctor."

"Okay Kevin, but I'm going to prove to you that you're wrong."
He left for work muttering, "You can prove it to yourself, I already know." As I approached the Doctor's office, I felt the nausea in my stomach. I rushed inside, barely making it to the toilet. I vomited. Finally, I managed to pull myself up, moved over to the sink to wash my hands and mouth. I glanced in the mirror, I looked pale. I dried my hands, and before long they were damp again. This was strange! I was hot one minute and cold the next. I felt faint!

When the medical assistant knocked on the door and saw me, she knew I needed emergency care. The doctor went ahead and took me. He examined me and told me that I was about six weeks pregnant. I was speechless. Beads of perspiration appeared on my face, and cramping pains penetrated my whole body. The doctor seeing the pain that I was undergoing asked, "Why are you torturing yourself like this? You seem really frightened and scared of the fact that you are pregnant. Would it make it any easier for you if you didn't have the baby?"

"That would be worse, I'll just have to deal with the consequences," I replied.

He gave me something to relieve the pain, and suggested that I sit in the waiting area for a while. He turned to his nurse, "You might want to check her blood pressure and make sure she gets some rest before leaving."

While driving home in the taxi, the fear of breaking the news to my mother scared me to death. The minute I arrived home, I dialed Larry.

"Larry, I just came home from the doctor and I am six weeks pregnant, how do you feel about that?"
"You're pregnant with my baby Nora? Are you sure it's my baby?
"What do you mean Larry? You took my virginity and now you're wondering if

you are the father of my baby? Whose baby could it be then?"

"Nora I'm just kiddin' I feel like a real man now knowin' that my seed has finally landed on fertile ground."

"Whatever Larry, but seriously are you okay with this though?"

Nora, it's the best news I've heard. I can hardly wait to see you, we'll talk more about it later on this evening."
"Larry, today is Tuesday, it's not Friday yet."
"Nora, I realize that, but don't you think this should be a time of celebration for us both? I should be there around six o'clock."

I hung up the phone feeling much better.
'Thank God he had proposed to me before I became pregnant, so I know he won't be marrying me, just because of the baby.'
I breathed a sigh of relief. Then and there, I dedicated myself to that man for the rest of my life, yet that bond had been created from the first time we made love. Then I thought, 'No wonder this is so important to me, Papa was the only man for Mama.'

When Larry arrived that evening, I took a long good look at him, and accepted him as the father of my child and also as my partner for life. He knew the challenge I faced as far as breaking this news to my mother.

"Baby, don't worry, I'll take care of it. We'll just kill two birds with one stone and inform them that we'll be getting married in July."
Shocked at this news, I remarked, "We are?"
"Didn't you expect that marriage would be the next thing in line Nora? Well there's no time like the present, and you'll be my bride before you know it."

Kevin was not at all surprised when he heard. Amazingly, he helped to lighten my burden and promised to break the news to Mama. As I anticipated, my mother took it very hard.

"Why couldn't you be like your sister Janice, and remain a virgin until you got married? Desmond and herself dated for four long years, and still, she kept herself pure. But you, you had to be the one to break the mould. Why have you brought this shame on us Nora? I don't know if I'll ever be able to live this down."

I became remorseful and attempted to tell her I was sorry. The intimidation I felt was scary, but I was determined to make peace with my mother. I mustered some courage, and slowly moved towards her,

"Mama I am truly sor…"

I was getting ready to embrace her, when she pulled away.

"No, do not touch me, because you're unclean."

I stood frozen. Eventually I retraced my steps and sat down, hurting as though my heart was being torn apart.
'How could she be so cruel,' I thought. 'I'm trying to say I'm sorry, and she won't even let me touch her. What more can I do?'

I pulled myself together as I tried to focus on what Papa was saying.
"Nora, my dream for you was to become a teacher, I doubt it very much if you'll be able to follow through on this, but I must admit that I'm a little disappointed. Only God knows why things have turned out this way. Maybe this child might be a special blessing in your life, so be encouraged and remember that you'll always have a place in my heart."

Tears of joy came to my eyes 'Why couldn't Mama have said at least one kind thing? I always knew that Mama was much firmer than Papa, so why was I so surprised?'

Then Larry, the eloquent speaker, took the floor.

"Mr. & Mrs. Harding, I regret that it is under these circumstances that I am conveying the deep seated love and respect that I have for your daughter. Frankly speaking, being a few years her senior, I have had several opportunities to interact with other women, but I must say that no one to this date has measured up to her qualities. Her strong Christian upbringing has given her a very solid foundation. I stand amazed when I see the way she handles the day-to-day challenges of life, so calm and with such a firm belief that things will work out. Please be understanding of her situation. I will love her and will father this child, and any others, with which the Lord will bless us. I am officially asking for Nora's hand in marriage Mr. & Mrs. Harding, and I can assure you that you can entrust her to my care. The good Lord brought her into my life, to teach me the true meaning of love. Finally, I must commend you on the fine job you have done parenting such a sincere, loving and special lady, soon to be my wife."

Papa remained quiet for a while, then got to his feet.
"Mr. Bell I must admit that I was really moved by your speech. Now to respond to

your request, under the circumstances I will immediately agree for you to marry my daughter, but I do wish the situation was a little different. It is very important that you listen to me very clearly. We have always lived in this part of the country, in fact a lot of Jamaicans are not even aware that this place exist. However, from these bushes have sprung, four beautiful rose buds, my daughters. You are very fortunate and blessed to be receiving one of them. Now, do not forget that she is a rose bud and I want you to treat her as one."

Try as I could, Mama's words were echoing in my ears, so I felt like going some place, just to get away to be by myself, to cry. I discreetly slipped through the back door, and went down to the gully. I sat under a banana tree and wept. I knew Mama loved me, but I didn't think she had to be so unforgiving. I knew I needed to forgive her, so through my tears I cried, asking God's forgiveness, for both Mama and myself. I was distracted by the sounds of footsteps on the dry, crisp banana leaves. I did not look up, as I quietly wished that it was Mama. A warm embrace from behind, and I turned around to face Kevin.

"Nora, I know that I've been very hard on you also, but it's because we had developed this bond, and I can't help but care for you. Leave the wedding up to me, I'll get the rest of them to help out with the money and you'll have a fabulous wedding. Please don't cry anymore Nora, everything will be okay."

We hugged, then walked back to the house together. Next it was Larry's turn to inform his father that we were getting married, and also about the pregnancy.

After we had spoken to him, his father turned to me and said, "If you lie with dogs, you'll get up with fleas."

I tried to understand what he meant, but it eluded me, and I let it go.

CHAPTER FIVE

I had gone to many weddings, but I never paid much attention to the wedding vows. My vows seemed so different, yet, they were the same ones I heard time and time again. These were serious, solemn, sacred vows. I quietly pledged that I was in this for the long haul, and like my parents I would abide by these vows 'till death do us part.'

Suddenly I had been transformed from a single woman to a wife, from the responsibility of my father to that of a virtual stranger, whose seed was growing inside me. I was dressed differently from all other brides, no long veil, no lace, no garters. I was dressed in a simple white caftan, with beads below the breast and around the neck. This was accompanied by a matching head wrap. My face wore no make up.

'How virginal,' I thought, smiling ironically, yet sadly. Although this was a happy day, it would be much happier if I had gone to take my vows chastened. I reflected on my past, but was uncertain as to what our future would be like, together. There was one thing I was sure of, I was committed and dedicated to Larry for the rest of my life.'

Our honeymoon was a brief one-night stop at a hotel in the city. But being pregnant took away from the magic and mystique that is usually shared by newly weds. Larry had secured a house for our residence in rural Jamaica, relatively close to his hometown. After our honeymoon he anxiously hurried to my house to collect my belongings to begin our journey together as a family. Kevin, Denise and my high school friend, Dawn accompanied us to the country. Kevin and Vanessa especially, had a keen interest in ensuring that my living conditions were appropriate.

The house was plain, furniture sparse, but comfortable. It consisted of a bedroom set and a dining room table with four chairs. Larry's stereo was stored on building blocks. The scantiness in the house was adequately compensated for, by the vast number of wedding gifts we had received. As we opened our presents, I experienced some mixed emotions. Suddenly, a feeling of loneliness swept over me, I was saddened when I realized that I'd be parting with Vanessa and Kevin soon. Deep within me was emptiness and I felt unsure about my future with Larry. These feelings intensified as my family drove away, leaving me behind.

The following morning I awoke to fix breakfast. While preparing the meal I noticed it was getting late and Larry was still sleeping. I went to the bedroom and shook him, trying to wake him up.

"Larry, Wake up! It's time to get up for work. It's already past eight o'clock, and you should've been at the office from seven forty five for your sales meeting. Larry, you're late."

Larry grumbled, "Let me give you a friendly warning. The worst thing a woman can do is to nag me. I will not tolerate it. If you wake me once and I'm not ready to get up, leave me the hell alone. I will get up on my time. Remember, before you moved in here, I was getting up for work. So it's in your best interest not to push me, because I guarantee, you will not like my response."

I went back to the kitchen and continued preparing breakfast when Larry staggered in.

"It's such a good feeling to wake up and have breakfast already prepared. You've made my day. By the way were you able to iron my shirt and get my clothes ready for work?"

"No, not yet. You can go ahead and eat, and I'll prepare your clothes in the meantime."

"Perfect."

While I ironed his shirt, I lost my appetite for breakfast. I couldn't wait for him to leave, so I could try and figure out what I really wanted to do with my life. After Larry ate, he left the dirty plate and utensils on the table.

"Nora, that was so good, I'm already looking forward to dinner. Don't forget the clothes in the hamper."

He hurriedly dressed for work and left.

I was alone and somewhat nervous so I began my chores to keep my mind occupied. I went in the bathroom and opened the hamper filled with dirty clothes. I sighed again. 'I feel as if I'm doing a day's work, I've got the whole day already planned for me. First, I have to clean the house then launder and iron the clothes, just like Mama's housekeeper. I wonder how long this will take me, since I've never done it before. Next, I have to prepare dinner and have it ready by the time Larry gets home, after he eats I'll have to clean up. And depending on Larry's mood, chances are, we'll have to have sex a couple times before he goes to sleep. Ahhhh…What a condition. Is this what married life is all about?'

Later that evening Larry came home from work totally exhausted.
"Darling I know you've got the dinner ready and waiting, I can't wait to eat."

He proceeded to undress in the kitchen, so by the time he got to the bedroom he was virtually naked. He quickly changed in something comfortable, and returned to the table, ready for his meal. With his mouth filled, he asked, "So did you manage to get all the laundry done today?"

I felt like answering, 'Yes Master,' but I took a deep breath and replied, "Yes Larry, I did."
I think he sensed my disgust, so he inquired about my day.

"Did you have a chance to rest at all?"

"Not really, I had so much to do." Before I was through answering, he interrupted.
"Don't worry, you'll soon have everything under control."

After eating, he got up from the table, sat in front of his stereo, with his headphones on. He loved his music, and from its soothing effect, and a full stomach, he'd fall asleep for hours and usually when he woke up it was time for sex.

'Imagine I've been home all day, yet, I've worked harder than this man. All that matters to him, is, food, music, and sleep. I only become a consideration, when he wants to have sex. There is absolutely no communication. How can we have a relationship if we hardly speak to each other? This is not a 'husband and wife, growing together type of situation, it is more like a master/helper, type thing. This was not what I bargained for! But on the other hand, maybe the fault lies with me, and he does not find me at all mentally stimulating. Whatever it is, I really hate to be ignored!'

As the weeks went by I began to notice a pattern. He was coming in later, and later each night. I wanted to address this matter, but the minute he got to the door, I'd get cold feet and abandon the thought of confronting him. It took me approximately four weeks before I could build up the courage to approach Larry.

I couldn't bear it any longer, and when he opened the door about 4:00 AM one Friday morning, I was sitting up in bed crying,

"Larry where have you been?"

His response came with a wild stare, and anger permeated his whole being, "Look woman, as long as I wear the pants in this house, you never, ever inquire about my whereabouts again."

I was growing to hate him, but I still somehow managed to love him. I resented the fact that I was being taken for granted, because I desperately needed his attention!

Larry and I drove into the city once per week for my doctor's visits, as the time was getting close for my delivery. It was a cool December evening, and after Dr. Jagaroon examined me, he suggested that I stay in the city, and wait for the baby's arrival. I quickly reflected on the story of my birth, and remembered how risky it was for Mama to travel to the hospital in the city, in that advanced state of pregnancy. I was not about to take any chances, so I decided to remain close to the hospital. Fortunately, I was packed and ready for the birth of the baby since I'd been six months pregnant. That same night, I was awakened by very sharp pains. When they started I wondered if I could live through them. They were excruciating, almost unbearable. Larry rushed me to the hospital, as the pains steadily increased.

Despite my own pain I could not help chuckling even as the incessant pains culminated into a sharp crescendo. My entire body was on fire. A fire that gradually bore down, and down, then one last surge, and finally – JOY! The pain turned into real joy, as I heard the cries of my first born, a son, reacting to the doctor slapping his tiny buttocks.

My baby, seven and a half pounds, healthy and well. Larry had remained in the room to witness the birth, so he came and stood by me.

"Nora you're a strong woman, and having an opportunity to observe my son's birth today, has allowed me to see you in a different light. Never in my wildest dreams did I imagine that this was such a painful experience. I'm thrilled I was able to share these precious moments with you and today I renew my commitment to you Nora. I will always be there for you and this child."

He was so sincere. I loved him, but just in case he went back on his word I now had my little pumpkin. I decided to name him after my little friend, who I'd taught in kindergarten. After suggesting it to Larry, we both agreed to name the baby Julius.

I had eagerly awaited the birth of this child, hoping that he would fill the gap in my increasingly lonely life and become my friend. I quietly hoped that Julius could help to fill the void in his father's life also, so he could find a reason to spend more time at home.

A few months later we moved to a larger home, in a quiet, middle-class area. This house was situated on a hill, with a magnificent view of the ocean. We had three bedrooms. Julius had his own, which was beautifully decorated with Sesame Street wallpaper. As he grew older his Dad had an oversized customized playpen specially built for him. This allowed Larry to hop in and play with the baby at times. On these occasions Larry would be so easy going, so amicable. The longer I lived with this man, the more I accepted the fact that I was involved with someone who had several different personalities. It was a little scary at times, because I was never sure what to expect.

As a new Mom, sometimes I would dress the baby and myself and go for walks in the neighborhood, while anxiously awaiting Larry's arrival from work. I tried my best to convey to him that I was a good mother and still an attractive wife, but not much appreciation was shown for either. One evening when he came home from work he was in a very strange mood, hardly talking, so I attempted to calm him.

"Did you have a bad day at work honey?
Is there anything I can do, to make you just smile?"

He shook his head and appeared disinterested in my efforts to help him be at ease.

"Let me just go ahead and serve dinner, I made your favorite dish so I know you'll be pleased. This should at least get you to say something like, 'Nora, if you keep cooking like this I'm going to start gaining weight."

After several unsuccessful attempts I decided to give it up, so we sat down to dinner. Poor Julius must have sensed the undercurrent, as he started crying uncontrollably. I pushed my chair back and moved to pick up the baby, but was stopped in mid motion by Larry's words. "Nora, don't you touch that damn child, you leave him alone and I will deal with him myself."

The sternness in his voice shocked me and left me frozen in the chair, staring across the table straight in his eyes.

"I'd suggest you stop staring at me like that, you might just wish you hadn't."

He gave me a daring look, pushed the table forward and his chair backwards. He picked up the baby, and carried him to the guestroom. He put him on the bed to lie on his stomach, while slapping his tiny bottom over and over again.

"You blasted spoilt brat, shut the hell up. I guarantee you'll sleep now. Just shut up and go to bed."

Julius was locked in the guest room where he bawled for hours. My heart was aching, yet I could not comfort my baby. Turning to me, he said, "I know you're thinking that I'm cruel, but remember the verse in Proverbs that says, 'Beat the child, it will not die.' So don't worry , your little brat will meet no harm."

It was my time to clam up, as I had no desire to respond. I hated him! Meanwhile, the cries from the room became weaker and weaker until they eventually died, so I assumed the poor thing finally fell asleep. Despite the tension, Larry turned on his charm.

"Nora, do you understand how much I love you, you mean everything to me, and strange as it may sound, that son of ours means a whole lot too. I don't regret anything I've done as far as it relates to Julius, but as for you, I really shouldn't treat you this badly. After all, you bring out the best in me. Come here baby, How about bringing out some of that stuff right now?"

He reached out to take me in his arms, but I retreated. I couldn't believe what I was hearing, "Larry, if you and I are thinking about the same thing, the answer is NO. Not under these conditions. Moreover, we've already had sex twice today. Doesn't your supply ever get low?"

"Good try Nora, that's not exactly funny, but I'll prove to you that I've got a built in reservoir."

Before I knew it, I was led like a lamb to the slaughter, with no way of escape. Larry grabbed me, pulled me down on the bed, unbuttoned my pants and tore off my underwear and before long he was pounding me relentlessly. All throughout this act, Larry seemed totally detached from the incident with the baby. This was not love making, it was simply a forceful screw.

When his snores confirmed that he was sleeping, I jumped up, pulled on a housecoat, and hurried to check on Julius. There he was, exhausted, soaking wet from perspiration. I bent over him, kissed his brows and as I changed his clothes scorching tears rolled down my cheeks unto his belly. I wiped the tears with his little Mickey Mouse sleepers in which I had dressed him. I gently picked him up and held him to my breast assuring him of my love. There were red blotches all over his face, from the prolonged agony. Half asleep, little Julius opened one eye, with an innocent look on his face, as if to say, 'I believe you care.'
Absolute tenderness filled my heart "J, I love you very much, and if this continues, you and I will run away one of these days, and your father will never ever see us again."

Then I thought of what I whispered to Julius about running away. I knew if I ever tried it, I would be made to pay the ultimate price…Maybe…
'Was it worth it?' I didn't think it was.
So reluctantly I dismissed the thought.
Trapped in Love? Hate?
Painfully I sighed and tried to sleep.

CHAPTER SIX

I had grown accustomed to Larry making all the major decisions, so he decided it was time for me to resume work. He approached his sister, who worked in a bank, to assist me in finding a job as a teller. She helped me secure the job, and I was given some time to find a helper, and get myself situated. Larry's cousin was hired to work for us. I stayed home for a few weeks to break her in, and to see how she'd cope, especially with Julius. During this time, it was customary for Larry to drop in for lunch, unannounced...Not just to satisfy his hunger, but also to quench his sexual urges. I found this situation uncomfortable, as it was obvious what was taking place.

When he sensed my uneasiness, he reminded me of the scriptures:
'The woman's body belongs to the man, and the man's body belongs to the woman.'He knew that since I had a strong Christian upbringing, I'd always adhere to the teaching of the scriptures. Although sometimes my own sexual needs were fulfilled, there were other times when I felt used, as if I was a vessel, a slave to my husband's needs, desires and fantasies. This realization was becoming really difficult for me to accept, and I was convinced that I needed an escape.

'Work could be a possible solution,' I thought.

So I went to the bathroom and practiced applying some makeup. I had not worn makeup for over a year, so I thought entering the workplace was the ideal time to make myself look more attractive. But when Larry opened the door, and saw my face all made-up, he went into a violent rage.

"What the hell is all this about, all these months that you've been home, I've never seen you wear make-up, and now that you're going out to work, all of a sudden you're taking on this new look? You will not leave this damn house with any blasted makeup on! My father always told me that whenever a woman makes a sudden change for no apparent reason, it's one of two things. It's either, she has another man, or she's looking for one. Which one is it Nora? Which one is it?"

Without giving me a chance to respond, he continued,"Let me give you a friendly warning, I will serve time, I will kill his ass without even thinking about it, so don't even entertain the thought. After all, you don't need that shit. It's only insecure people have to resort to wearing that crap. Remember, it was your natural beauty that attracted me in the first place. So I'd suggest we keep it that way."

He continued, anyway, the reason I came in here was to tell you that I've been offered a job to become a sales rep for one of the leading insurance companies."I didn't feel like talking to him but I needed to get one question answered.

"So let me ask you this, is this job paying you a salary or is it straight commissions?"

He didn't respond so I continued.

"I remember when Frederick got into the Insurance Industry, some months he would make a killing and there were months he could enlist on the pauper's role. I'm not trying to be negative an all, but remember you've got a family now, and the risk factor is very great."

He looked at me as if to say. 'If it takes me all evening, I will not stop until I convince you.' So he responded.

"Nora, they're offering me a base pay, during the four week of training. After which time, I'll become a licensed agent. By the way, the weekly salary works out to be about 50% more than I'm making right now. After the training I will receive a draw against commissions for three months. However, when I'm fully trained and licensed, I'll go on straight commissions. Nora I've got nothing to lose, and everything to gain. This will be my last week with the food distribution company, as I'm scheduled to start the new job next Monday."

The following Monday, Larry started his new career and within four weeks we made a major status change and moved into our dream house. Larry had been breaking every record with the Insurance Company, and was making a lot more money than he was accustomed to. We afforded ourselves the luxury of two full time helpers, one was assigned to take care of Julius and preparing the meals, while the other did the usual household chores. A boy came in every other day to trim the lawn and to ensure the upkeep of the quarter acre land. In this quiet surrounding, I prayed that peace would finally enter our lives, similar to the tranquil clear blue waters, ebbing and flowing outside. Larry was very pleased with his progress, and thought that it was an opportune time to re-enroll in the military.

"Nora, I've been doing a lot of thinking lately and I'm quite satisfied with our lifestyle and our accomplishments. But whenever I think about the army, I feel really empty. My goal of becoming an army officer was unfulfilled. I hate this feeling. It's one of defeat and the only way to regain my self worth is to start at the bottom and prove to myself and others, that I am not a quitter. I must finish what I started, or else my life will have no meaning. No matter how much money I make, it will never be able to compensate.

With renewed determination, he enrolled in the army as a reserve, starting out as a private soldier. He was very motivated as he worked towards his goal of becoming an army officer. Having gone through the army before, Larry was able to achieve his goal in record time. One Year.

He became a lieutenant and served part time with the Jamaican army. During the training period his personality underwent various changes. I was not about to question him, since achieving this goal meant more to him than life itself. I understood the importance that was placed on rebuilding his self-worth. But once the goal was achieved I took a closer look, and I observed a stern, serious, deep and unpredictable army officer. Another one of his personalities was that of an over achiever, who was highly motivated, goal driven and portrayed the successful corporate executive. A third personality was that of an arrogant and moody martial artist who was eager to learn and master the power of the mind. This disposition was a little scary, as more times than not the meditation adjusted his behavioral pattern.

Although my husband was very busy with his regular job at the Insurance Company along with all his other involvements, he still found time to visit the night clubs. When I confronted him he rationalized his actions.

"Nora all I'm doing is taking out a few hours for me. Do you understand the hectic lifestyle that I lead? A little music and some drinks make a world of difference."

"Larry, I really think you need to slow down. You're only human, and if you continue like this one of these days you're going to break. With the long hours you're putting in, you don't need alcohol to soothe your nerves. An addiction to alcohol will cut your manhood and if I think I know you the way I do, I don't think you could live with that."

"One thing I can assure you of, alcohol can never interfere with my sexual drive so watch what you're saying. I frankly don't care about what effect alcohol has on other men, but as far as I'm concerned that does not apply to me. By the way, if you have any doubts about my sexual abilities, I'd be more than happy to put your doubts to rest. Right now."He challenged me.

"Listen, I'm not in the mood tonight. There're a lot of things going on in my mind that I couldn't even focus on that right now."I responded.

"I hope you realize you're turning me down so if I have to go elsewhere to satisfy my desires, I trust you'll be able to deal with it."He flaunted.

"Larry whatever….I'm just not in the frame of mind for sex tonight."

"All right baby, your loss may be another woman's gain."
With that he left the room and I fell off into a fitful sleep.
As the sun's rays flooded the room I heard the jangling of house keys. Larry stumbled into the room, reeking of alcohol and passed out on the bed. This incident heightened my insecurity, and I knew his womanizing intensified. I was uncertain what direction to take, and the solution I thought, was to have another child. Julius was constantly begging for a baby brother and at the rate at which we made love, this was a no-brainer.

During this second pregnancy, I realized that Larry was having several affairs. I confronted him and he became very arrogant.

"Listen woman, all you need to know is that I'm coming home to you, and I'm not taking anything from my immediate family to sustain an outside relationship. Back off and give me a break. Let me just inform you once and for all that I'm in demand out there, and you should be lucky that you're the one wearing my ring. There are numerous women who would do anything in their power to have me. So count your lucky stars."

Fool that I was, I settled for that, and thought for a minute that I was fortunate to have Larry. I was resigned to demeaning myself and concentrated on bearing my second child.

CHAPTER SEVEN

Around that time I noticed an addition to his multiple personalities. He was becoming very interested in religion, and had begun an intense search for truth within the bible. He stayed up night, after night exploring the scriptures. One morning when I woke up, I noticed all the wine and alcoholic beverages had been removed from the liquor cabinet.

"Larry what happened? Did you consume all this alcohol?" I inquired.

"Woman, don't be ridiculous. As of this day, I do not wish to have any type of liquor in my system. My body is the temple of Jesus Christ, and I will not poison it with alcohol. God has commanded me to get rid of all the alcohol in this house, and I emptied every last drop in the kitchen sink last night. The damaging effects of alcohol consumption have been revealed to me, and I will have no part of it. Just go ahead and throw out the empty bottles, as the subject is not debatable."

"Larry you're speaking to me Nora, have you ever seen me drink alcohol. Don't mix me up with your drinking partners. Alcohol means nothing to me."

He moved over to me and placed his hand on my stomach.
"Nora I have to do this for all of us, it's important that I set a good example. But on a slightly different note, your stomach has gotten huge. How many months are you now?"

"Larry I know you're busy, but I thought you knew that I'm almost nine months pregnant. The baby can come any time now."

Holding his head down. "God I feel bad, I had no idea you were this far gone. But do me a favor and get your things together so I can take you and Julius to your brother. That way you'll be close to the hospital."

It was late the next evening when Larry drove Julius and I from the country, to stay with Orette and his family in the city. Julius and I had our own room and bathroom, we settled in quite nicely, and despite my discomfort, I enjoyed the time away from Larry. Their helper was at my beck and call, and I was not allowed to lift a straw, so I was stress free.

Friday morning I was awakened by Julius, "Mommy you're alright? Why are you crying Mommy?"

"Mmmmmmm," was my only reply.

"The baby want to come out?" He asked.

I smiled sleepily, then immediately, I felt a sharp pain. Lying flat on my back, I turned my face to the wall, so he couldn't see the painful expression on my face. I felt his little hands walking all over my stomach, as though he was getting ready to examine me.

"Mommy, I should carry my doctor kit, so I could check an tell you what's wrong, but I left it at home."
I smiled, as I listened to my son, he was too funny.

"Mommy, no more space is in your tummy for my brother, the doctor have to cut it today, and take him out."

"Ouch," I couldn't conceal the pain any longer.
Meanwhile, my little doctor brought his hands up to my face and turned my head away from the wall.

"Mommy don't cry, let me wake up Uncle Orette and tell him you have to go to the doctor right now."
As my niece assisted me in getting dressed for the hospital, she said.

"Aunt Nora, remember I want to name the baby, so please tell dad to call and tell me as soon as he's born."

Julius interrupted, "Mommy you're coming back with my brother today, right?"

I kissed him, "J, in a few days I'll return from the hospital with either a baby brother or sister, but the most important thing, is to take home a healthy baby."

As I slowly walked to the car with Orette, Julius rushed out,"Excuse me Mommy, but come back quick with my brother."
Despite the aches, I smiled and bent down to kiss him again,

"Mommy loves you very much darling, and I will try my best to bring home a brother for you."

My second child, a son, was born on November 7th, 1978. He entered the world at seven pounds, ten ounces. Now we didn't have a name. However, my niece was waiting for the call, so she could name the baby. She named her little cousin Luther, and both Larry and I were pleased. Julius, who was approaching his third birthday, had a special name for his brother.

He called his brother,'Mr. Bapps.' His reason, to this day, remains unknown.
We stayed at Orette's for another week. Then, we returned to our home in the country.

Julius watched his brother as if he was a military guard on duty. He only took a break to sleep, eat a mouthful and use the bathroom. Other than that, he was with Luther almost round the clock. It was as though he had some major plans that couldn't be implemented without the assistance of 'Mr. Bapps.' I became excited as I pictured them growing up together and enjoying the sunshine, the beach and this lovely house. I envisioned them playing on the patio without a care in the world, and experiencing true love. I was beginning to settle down to the role of a dedicated mother and a dutiful wife. Happiness had finally come, and I was going to hold onto it for as long as I could.

Soon it was time for me to return to work, and it was heartbreaking to leave my two boys. But my helpers were reliable, and I felt confident that I could depend on them. Before long, I settled in the routine of my job, and my enthusiasm and energy was back. I had a good rapport with both staff and customers, and I heard through the grape vine that I was next in line for a promotion. I looked forward to this, and waited with much anticipation for its announcement.

CHAPTER EIGHT

I returned fifteen minutes early from my lunch break, and was just in time to hear the secretary say, "Hold on Mr. Bell, please don't hang up she just walked in."

A feeling of tension came over me as the secretary put the call on hold, and addressed me, "Mrs. Bell, it's your husband. I'm not trying to alarm you but it sounds very important. He refused to hang up, so I hope everything's okay." I became even more tensed and hurriedly took the call.

"Larry, what's the matter? Are the boy's alright?"

"I spoke to the helper about thirty five minutes ago, and up to that time they were fine. Just relax, this is good news." He continued,

"I just received a call from my mother in the States, and she got her citizenship." He seemed extremely excited, "Nora she's going to be sponsoring all of us and we'll be leaving to live with my family in the States."

I was dumbstruck, and for a minute there was silence on the line. Then I managed to ask, "All of us who? Going where?"

"I'm assuming you didn't quite understand me, so let me try and say this another time. Larry, Nora, Julius and Luther Bell will be leaving Jamaica to live with my family in the United States soon. Was that simple enough?"

Even though I felt faint I replied, "How on earth can you take this upon yourself, and make such a major decision without us discussing it?"

"Look woman, don't get me upset. In this family I make the decisions, I don't

need prior approval from you. Here's the bottom line, you either migrate with us, or stay here with your family. Because I know you don't want to be separated from your boys."
I was conscious that my co-workers could hear what was being discussed so I politely replied,"Let's continue this conversation when we get home."I was about to hang up when I realized he was still talking.

"Again let me emphasize, this is not up for discussion. The decision has already been made."

I found it impossible to focus on work so I left an hour early. When we sat down to dinner that evening, I had no appetite. I was still in shock after the conversation with Larry. I resented the fact that I was alienated from such a decision.

Larry attempted to defend his stand."Nora, Jamaica is developing ties with Cuba and I believe it's on its way in becoming a communist nation. Do you realize, that when we migrate we can only leave the Country with $56.00 U.S. each, and if we attempt to smuggle out a dime more, we could be prohibited from leaving, and possibly serve a jail sentence? So I've come to the conclusion that it's in our best interest to migrate to the United States. My mother is a warm and caring person and she'll do her best to make you feel at home. I promise you'll not regret this move. I'm very confident that things will work out for the better. But it would help if you'd be a little more understanding."

I thought to myself, 'If he was such a committed army officer and was privy to all this information, why was he leaving at a time when his country needed him most?'

Then I turned to him and said, "Larry, the way I feel right now, is that living in Jamaica is a risk in itself, but migrating to the unknown is just as risky. The question is which is the greater of the two?"

We argued this point, with opposing views, but undoubtedly he won the argument. I became very subdued, left the dining room and headed for my bed. Defeated, I did what I knew best. Cried! With my head submerged in the pillow, I refused to look up when Larry walked in the bedroom.

The dictatorship continued, "I will have your letter of resignation written and ready to be handed in to your supervisor tomorrow. Are you with me?"

I choose not to respond, but as long as the night was, I could not sleep. I was afraid the confusion I was experiencing, would lead to mental crisis. I certainly did not want to go along with his plan, but I'd also made a commitment that only death would separate me from my children.

The following day after returning from work, Larry met me at the door. "By the way, you'll not be able to work tomorrow, because we'll have to wake up at the crack of dawn, to be at the registrar's office. We'll be looking about the passports and finally going to the American embassy to pick up the visas. Just in case you're not fully apprised in carrying out my orders, the boys must accompany us tomorrow. I suggest you take out their clothes, and get everything prepared from tonight."

He paused, then chuckled a bit, "Ah Nora, it has been said that the early bird catches the most worms, therefore we've got a lot to do. What we'll accomplish in one day, the average person needs six months to a year. I'll make the impossible, possible. I guarantee we'll be home by five tomorrow evening, with birth certificates, passports and visas. The only thing left is for us to purchase the tickets.

When he saw that I didn't respond, he became serious again.
"And while we're at it, I'd suggest that you do not go and broadcast around town that we're migrating. Because of my association with the army, we've got to be extremely discreet. You can go ahead and mention it to your family, but under no circumstances, must they be given specific details regarding the date and time of our departure."

As I started to get the kids clothes ready, it suddenly dawned on me what this man was asking me to do. I was so overwhelmed that I burst out crying. I spoke through the tears, "Listen, I've gone along with the plan so far, but my family has not done anything to deserve this disrespect. You're grossly unfair, because it's only your family that counts. I hate this feeling, and I hate you."

In a controlled tone, he replied, "You might very well hate me now, but you'll live to thank me later. And by the way, your tears mean absolutely nothing to me, but you'd better watch your mouth. Like I said, you're only allowed to mention it to your family, but under no condition, must they be given any details. And try to defy me on this Nora. I promise you'll regret it."

When we broke the news to my family, I gave them the impression that I was looking forward to the change. Larry had me under constant surveillance, so I wanted to shorten the visit and leave, as I couldn't be myself. My mother saw through the facade. I could tell she was worried about my situation, as she was unable to camouflage her feelings. Her concern was transmitted to my father, and

he questioned our decision.
"If you folks are doing so well, why are you leaving then?"

Papa was not through speaking, when Mama interrupted.
"And so suddenly too! Something is not right dear; something is not right with this picture."

Larry was becoming uneasy, and refused to be interrogated by my parents.

"Nora, we've got to go," he said.
As we got up to leave, Mama said to Papa.

"Dear, let us say a word of prayer for them before they leave, because I get the feeling that this family is going to need a lot of prayers."

She kissed her grandsons and barely said good-bye to Larry. I knew in my heart that they were very nervous, and they'd be praying for our protection. As I walked away from her and Papa she assured me that God would not give me more than I could bear.

Back at home, things were moving with whirlwind speed. Within three weeks we tried to sell an entire house of furniture and accessories, plus three cars. We were not very successful in doing so. When it was time for us to leave, we were forced to give away a lot of valuable items. This added to my depression.

Finally, we were at the airport getting ready to board. I held Luther while Julius walked beside me. As we entered the airplane, I fought back the tears. I swallowed hard as I was choked up. I glanced back at the sunshine and the clear blue skies. I was leaving the land of my birth, for a foreign land, without the semblance of a plan.

CHAPTER NINE

Larry's mother and sister met us at the airport. We had relatively little luggage since we were advised to travel lightly. We got through the airport formalities quickly.

"So you guys finally made it? Nora if you don't mind, let me take my grandson." I handed her the baby, "It's my pleasure ma'am because I'm very exhausted."

Turning to me, his sister asked, "So how was the flight?"
"It was alright I guess."

She took Julius's hand and we began to walk swiftly, it seemed as though someone was coming after us.

'We had to run from Jamaica, and we're here now, and we're still running. Maybe, this was truly an escape after all, but from what?'

At last we reached my sister-in-law's VW bus, and we all piled in. I was silent as we drove through the traffic filled streets of New York. It was still difficult for me to accept what was happening. I had imagined that, like Jamaica, the residential areas of New York would be in the hills, and definitely away from the hustle and bustle of the crowded city. I remained calm, as I continued my view of the city, anticipating the residential suburbs.
I imagined we'd have a good hour or so, before we reached our destination. But when Marion, my sister-in-law pulled up and parked next to the side walk, before a brown stone building, I thought she was making a stop to pick up something. I was utterly shocked when she announced.

"We're home at last guys. Welcome to Brooklyn."

Bitterly disappointed I looked at Larry, and under my breath I said.
'How could you have done this to us?'

He too could not conceal his frustration. We moved into a three bedroom house, with one bathroom, and a partially finished basement. There were eleven people already living there before we moved in and now there were fifteen. His family was very accommodating, and tried to keep the place as clean as possible, but it was just too crowded for me.

Flatbush Avenue was only a few blocks away, and the streets were always busy. I found it difficult to cope with the constant sounds of sirens, fire trucks, buses, and the whistling of the train. Larry was in a state of serious depression from the day we arrived. His despair worsened when he opened a sealed envelope, which was supposed to contain a few thousand dollars he'd smuggled out of the country. He had tipped off a police officer to assist him and when he was handed the envelope he was confident that it had the correct amount. To his disappointment the money was short a couple thousand dollars. This experience left him severely depressed. Yet, he was too proud to admit it.

Eventually there was progress, Larry got a temporary job as a security guard, and later obtained a permanent position as an insurance salesman with a reputable company. This enhanced his attitude, and did wonders for his self-esteem. I also found a job, with the help of a friend who resided in Jamaica. He had strong connections with the personnel department for the Regional bank. I was hired there as a teller, and was assigned to the Wall Street branch in Manhattan. At the time, I was the only black teller in that branch.

I immediately gained favor with my co-workers and many of my customers were intrigued with my accent. This was a challenging experience for me, and even though I hated the subways, I liked my job, and looked forward to it each day. I was committed to outstanding performance, and within three months, I was promoted to the head teller.

In the meantime Larry was finally settling in to the New York lifestyle, and was thrilled to be back in the limelight. Suddenly his work hours were extended to 2:00 and 3:00 AM in the mornings. I quietly observed. One Saturday morning after seeing lipstick all over his shirt I confronted him.

"Let me ask you a question Larry, is it that you don't know how to be discreet, or is it that you don't care?"

"I have told you time and time again, that I do not have to answer to you. Not even the woman who gave birth to me can question my whereabouts. So what makes you think that you can?"

It was hard for me to understand that someone who professed to love me could be so disrespectful and abusive. The shame I felt was intense, and I wanted to hide my pain and pretend that everything was alright. The complexity of my life with this man increased with each day.

CHAPTER TEN

The cool spring mornings slowly changed into summer, and I was finally able to take out some clothes, without having to worry about wearing the faded spring coat. One Thursday morning I decided it was time for my appearance to take on a transformation, like the weather itself. So I wore a close fitting pants suit, with a short jacket and matching shoes. My hair was not pinned back as usual, but was loose with the curls teased. The reflection from the mirror left a pleasant expression on my face.

'Despite what I'm going through I still look good, and I'm going to fight to maintain this confidence. It's almost impossible, to put my best out, when I'm hurting so miserably inside. But I'm determined to put my crosses behind me and move positively towards a brighter future, despite my situation.'

As I rode the train to work that morning I thought to myself. Larry, like most men, wants to have his cake and eat it too. It's about time I stand up to him, and stop being afraid. I will not let him 'rain on my parade.' From this day on I will exude positivity and somewhere down the road I will attract the right energy and hopefully, the right man!'

Later at the bank, Dexter a customer who I sensed was attracted to me came up to my window, although I'd posted a closed sign.
"Excuse me Nora, what time do you go for lunch?"
Shocked at his inquiry I abruptly replied, "Why?"

Taken aback with my response, he explained, "I was only inviting you to join me for lunch today. But I'm sorry if I offended you."
I wanted to cry. I had no reason to be rude, but that's how controlled I was. I lost my assertiveness and was acting rather silly.

"I don't even know if I can....I---'m not sure what I'm doing today. I---I don't know!"
I lost control. Lost my nerves and sounded as though I'd lost my mind.

I felt insecure. He was very handsome, a quiet mannered black male, and extremely polite, about 5' 11" tall. His skin was free from blemish, and was smooth as a newborn baby. He might have been in his late twenties, and he was gorgeous. As I watched him enter the elevator, I secretly wished that I could 'turn back the hands of time' and say yes to his invitation. But I wouldn't dare! My reaction was caused by both fear and low self-esteem.

That evening when I got to the block where we lived and saw Larry's car, I was curious to know why he was home so early. Immediately I thought something was wrong.

I rushed to the bathroom to take a quick look at my face to see if it was reflecting any guilt as to my feeling of disloyalty. To my amazement, Larry was stooping over the tub giving Luther a bath. I almost passed out! This was a first time! It never happened before! 'I wondered what brought this on?'

For a moment, I thought he'd changed, and had now become the husband I always dreamed of. But being so unpredictable, he might very well be up to something. The latter lingered in my thoughts. Uncertain of how to greet him I finally said, "Larry how come you're home so early, and bathing Luther at that?"

"I've had a lot of time to think about how hard it must be on you, especially with me being so inconsiderate. I've decided to make some changes, and help out some more. Can't you see I'm serious about this commitment? Look, I'm bathing the baby. What more proof do you want? I promise from now, you'll see a change in me."

He was transformed to coy tenderness, and began to look me over with admiration. "Mmmmmmm. Despite what you're going through you still look good. You dressed exceptionally well today, what was the occasion?"

 I became uncomfortable with his line of questioning.
"Larry there was no special reason. It's just that I've been hurting a lot on the inside, and have been trying very hard to cover it up. But I've been unable to. Today I decided to improve my appearance and see if I could feel better, that's all."
"So did you feel better?" He asked.
"I sure did," I replied.

It seemed as though he was trying to figure out what his next bait should be. "Nora I really cannot help but admire this new look. I have to try and get accustomed to it."

He paused for a moment, "I'm sure your friend from the bank is finding you very attractive too. What's his name again?"

As though hypnotized by his gaze, I asked, "Who? Dexter?"

Cunningly he replied, "Yeah Dexter."

A fox like grin slowly spread across his face. He relieved himself of the baby and was back in the bathroom in a matter of seconds. He locked the door behind him. Circling me again and again, hands in pocket, gazing at his feet. Stooping in front of me he said, "Nora I've gone through this before, and you must understand that I'm your best friend, so you must feel comfortable to tell me everything. The love I have for you is so deep, that no matter what you do, I'll forgive you.

Do you realize how often you've forgiven me? Too many times to mention, now it's my turn to return the favor, so let it all out and let's talk about it. You'll be more than happy you did, because it will take a load off your back."

I was too astonished by his words, and his demeanor was too cool for me to respond. This was unlike his normal behavior. I became uneasy, but he did not let up, he continued his probing. "So, have you gone out to lunch with him as yet?"

He paused while he waited for my answer.
"No, I wasn't sure if it was right for me to go."

"But why wouldn't it be? I cannot see what could be so wrong with a man and woman going out for lunch. Now, if there is any type of intimacy between both parties, then that's an entirely different story. Come on Nora, level with me. Do you like this guy in an intimate way?"

I wasn't sure how to respond, as I wanted to answer correctly. There was a lengthy silence, and I thought if I told Larry what he wanted to hear, he'd let me off. So feeling spellbound, I timidly replied, "Yes. I think I do."

Again he circled me, "I know this may be hard for you to tell me, especially being your husband, but how do you feel when you imagine him making love to you? It's an exciting feeling, isn't it?"

I did not respond, and he continued, "Look Nora, it's only a fantasy, so don't think you're doing anything wrong. It's quite normal to feel this way. I have a lot of fantasies, and I enjoy them all. The greatest one I have is to be able to make love to two women at the same time. I bet you didn't know that."

"I suspected it, but I wasn't really sure." I replied.
Nora I've leveled with you so don't be afraid to share your secrets with me,
remember, I'm not your enemy."

This weird cross questioning started around 7:00 PM, in the bathroom. Hours
later, it was transferred to the bedroom. And approximately 4:00 AM it was still
in full force. I was not even allowed a bathroom break. By the time he had
completed his interrogation I was convinced that not only had I gone to lunch
with Dexter, but I'd also gone to bed with him.

Later that morning as I got ready for work both my mind and my body were
drained. I felt very nervous and uncertain about my life. In one corner of my
mind I was almost sure that I had been involved with Dexter, while in another
corner I was cautioned.

'You're right at the brink, but remain strong. This is an invasion of your brain!
This is a strategy to let you believe you're guilty, when you're not. Your husband
is trying to drive you crazy, but remember don't fall for it!'

Then I remembered the words of my mother, 'Nora I will be praying for you
everyday, because I feel that this family is going to need a lot of prayers.' As I
walked swiftly down Wall Street I whispered another prayer.

"Lord please impress on Mama, that I'm desperately in need of constant prayers
today."

When I entered the bank I tried to act composed, but my co-workers sensed
that I was not my normal self. Early that afternoon, I told my supervisor that I
wasn't feeling well and requested to leave, so I could get some rest. I went home
in trepidation. I knew I could never go through another night like last night. As
I looked out the train window at the receding tracks, I felt like jumping out and
putting an end to all this misery, all the crosses. Then I asked myself.

'But who'd be there for Julius and Luther? No one! Larry was not the type of
father who would be committed to see to the well being of his children.'

Once more as I turned the corner, and headed towards home, I saw Larry's car,
parked right by the gate. This was uncanny! I was nervous and afraid to face
another night of fear and mental torture.
Quietly I cried, 'God, please don't let me end up in a mental institution, just let me

remain sane for my children.'
A gloom hovered over the house, and it seemed like the entire place was painted black. Suddenly I felt the urine slowly seeping through my off black panty hose, and I ran to the bathroom, to finish emptying my bladder.

As I rushed to take off my stockings, Larry barged in.
I was in for trouble!
I was caught red-handed!
Now he had evidence! My wet panties and pantyhose!
I was guilty! It was written all over my face. There was nothing I could say to convince Larry that I was innocent.

His eyes were blood red as though he'd been smoking marijuana. He gave me one of his deadly stares. He grabbed me from behind with one hand around my neck, and the other over my mouth. I was choking, but couldn't cough or scream. In a deep husky voice he berated me.

"You slut, think I wouldn't catch you? Did you go to a hotel, or to his place?"

His grip tightened around my neck and I thought he was going to strangle me. I shuddered, when I remembered that he almost strangled his former girlfriend with a belt, when she left him for another man. Still squeezing my neck he said.

"I've a good mind to kill you right here, but I must torture you first. Because, you've kept another man with me, and you must pay."

I was terrified to death, but I silently prayed for the Lord to have mercy and deliver me from this crazed man. Suddenly a look of frustration overcame him, and it was as if his hands were miraculously removed from my neck.

"I'm not sure what's happening to me, but I can't do this."
He shoved me in the corner and left me trembling. When I suddenly regained my strength, I ran out of the bathroom, downstairs to the kitchen, where his mother was. She found it difficult to deal with the situation, as it only brought back bitter memories of her past. I could sense the dread in her voice, as she grabbed his arm begging.

"Please Larry don't hurt her, remember the children."

That only added more venom to his adrenaline. He rushed over to the refrigerator and with one massive punch he made a large dent. I looked at him and when our eyes met, I realized that it wasn't the right time to stare in his blood-shot eyes.

I sensed death. Vengeance was written all over his face, and I felt my end was near.

He removed a knife from the sink and moved towards me with tremendous force, aiming the weapon towards my heart. Suddenly, his cousin, a big guy over six feet tall, rushed in, grabbed his hands, holding them behind his back until he dropped the knife.

I remained with my back to the wall, feeling almost lifeless, and uncertain as to whether or not I'd been pierced. I was numb. Yet, my consciousness cried out to God. Despite the intervention, Larry was still very angry, and in an effort to vent his anger he thrust his bare fist in the wall, leaving a huge hole. He was on a rampage, and he was committed to destroy everything around him, but I was the main target.

What he experienced I do not know, but once again, God came to my rescue. He took a long look at me, shook his head and left through the front door.

I went to my room, exhausted and trembling as though waking from a seizure. My thoughts were confused and it was impossible to focus. I needed to speak with my family. I reached for my little black book, and nervously searched for my brother's number. Tavaris resided in Queens, New York. I finally found his number and made about six attempts before dialing it right.

"Hello Tavares."

I was speaking very quietly because I was afraid Larry could be lurking in the dark, listening to my conversation. I knew he'd not have wanted me to call him.

"Who is this? Whoever you are, I cannot hear a word you're saying and I'm much too busy for games."

"It's Nora. Can you hear me now? It's me. Nora."

"Nora what is wrong with you?" The minute I realized that my brother had recognized my voice, I broke down and cried, and not another word could come from my lips. I was due for a good cry, and that I did.

In less than forty-five minutes I heard the doorbell ring. It was Tavares. We embraced, and he assured me that Mama's prayers had saved my life. He gave me some sound advice, and as we spoke, Larry entered the room. Tavares was fuming and before he could say a word, Larry stated his case.

"I know you're going to want to leave with your brother, but I'm the problem and I need to remove myself from the situation. You and the boys can stay here with Mom. I'll leave tonight."

He went to the closet and began to take down his clothes, and before long he was completely packed. He turned to Tavares, "Listen I don't need to explain anything to you, but I'm leaving so your sister will be safe."

"You do not deserve my sister, I hope one day she will have the guts to put you behind bars."

Turning to me he said, "Nora please call the cops if he tries to hurt you or the kids." He assured me of his love, gave me some money, then left.

Larry went away that night, but his packed suitcase remained in the corner of the living room. I didn't like that, but I was too afraid to ask any questions. I returned to the privacy of my room, needing to be by myself. I thanked God for preserving my life, and keeping me safe. I tried to formulate a plan, something that would be in the best interest of me and my boys, but nothing materialized. Suddenly around midnight the door was thrust open, and Larry entered the bedroom.

My heart pounded and I became hysterical. I was afraid, and was even willing to sleep with him, if that would've spared me from the mental torture. In a shrill voice I turned to him and asked, "Do you want to sleep with me tonight?"

He remained silent, then moved towards me, faced me and very, very, coldly replied, "Nora, I do not want your body as a peace offering."

How much more cruelty could I endure at this man's hands, and still retain my sanity? I felt such shame. His remark cut me to the ground. 'How much more Lord? How much more?'

CHAPTER ELEVEN

Quietly and determinedly, I went on a cleaning campaign, not resting as I was uncertain what could happen if I slept. Larry returned home and unpacked all his clothes. For as long as he was up, I worked, and long after he went to sleep I remained awake. I was really afraid to sleep since I felt I had to keep my guards up. I did not trust him.

He had become very withdrawn and quiet after his games of interrogation and intimidation. He spent a lot of time sorting papers and writing documents, but I was not at all interested to know what he was doing. As I dressed for work on Monday morning he came in the room.

"Nora I'd like for you to give this to your supervisor today, because this will be your last week at the bank."

He read the letter and then handed it to me. It was my resignation! I remained quiet, and stared at him in disbelief. He looked at me, and said."There's nothing for us to talk about. Just make sure your supervisor gets it, the minute you walk in."

Hesitantly I replied,"No problem, I will."

After a brief train ride through the city I arrived at the bank. I handed in my letter of resignation, and tried to convince everyone that it was a mutual decision between my husband and I. That weekend they had a send-off party for me, and a few of the customers were invited. I wished Dexter could have been among the guests, so I could tell him the price I had to pay for his invitation to lunch. At the end of the evening I had many gifts and cards from my co-workers. We all embraced and said good-bye, hoping that one day we'd somehow meet again.

Larry was pleased to know that I did as he commanded. He became calm and caring. I began to trust him again, and before long, we were back to a pleasant and warm relationship. Despite his hectic schedule, he sacrificed time to pursue his favorite sport, the martial arts. When he was not training, he'd put on his karate uniform and go through the routine warm up exercise in the house.

He'd bought Julius his own little karate uniform, and spent sometime breaking him into the marital arts. One evening after he was through working with Julius, he came upstairs, and said to me, "Nora I'm really concerned about you not knowing how to defend yourself. Moreover, as your husband, it's my responsibility to teach you. So if you don't mind, put on one of my jogging pants, and a loose top, and I'll give you some basic lessons."

"Is that really necessary?" I asked.

Yet, he insisted, "All you've got to do is just tell yourself that you're going to do it, and you'll be surprised to see how easy it will be for you to get in the frame of mind. Just give it a try, please."

"Okay, I'll meet you downstairs as soon as I get dressed."
He seemed pleased that he'd convinced me.

"Nora this evening I'm going to teach you several self defense techniques. The first demonstration involves an attacker carrying a weapon. The most common way of attacking a victim is from behind. Because an attack is never planned and always unexpected, victims often panic out of fear of losing their lives. The purpose of this training is to teach you how to get the attacker to break his hold or to get him distracted and lose his focus, so you can escape. When I hold you like this, can you move?"

He grabbed my throat as he had days earlier. I was scared but did not let it show. What was his real intention? As he demonstrated the technique, I tried to get out of his hold but couldn't. I panicked. Is he trying to kill me? My heart pounded. My arms failed.

"Nora what are you doing?"

He released his hold. I was dazed and confused. Then, unexpectedly he lunged toward me. I fell and hit my coccyx right on the edge of the wooden stairs. It all happened so fast, but what happened? The pains were excruciating.

"Now I really feel bad," he said, as he chuckled to himself. He could not have known the extent of my pains.

"Here I am, teaching you how not to get hurt, and you end up hurting yourself. This is crazy! It's the last thing I expected to happen. This was certainly not my intent. Nora I'm sorry."

But the pains did not let up. They steadily increased.
"Nora do you think you broke anything? I think I'd better take you to the doctor. At least we will know for sure what happened."
In pain I replied, "Yes please do."

At the doctor's office a series of x-rays were done, and the results indicated that the coccyx, the main bone resting at the tip of the spine, was cracked. No wonder the pains were so piercing. He gave me something to ease the pain, and recommended a lot of bed rest. He suggested that I stay away from all types of exercise and activities including sex.

The days following my visit to the doctor were awful. No matter what I did my body felt strange. The pains in my back were severe and sporadic, but at the same time, I was having some serious cramps in my stomach.

'Maybe it's all this medication I'm taking, but somehow, I still don't feel right.'

After a long debate with Larry, I decided to see my gynecologist. He would be able to shed light on the situation.

To my surprise after a thorough examination he announced.
"Mrs. Bell you're approximately seven weeks pregnant."
This was the last thing I expected to hear.

"Doctor, are you positive? Can you please double check to make sure?" I was hoping against all odds that he was wrong. "I can't believe those results are right."

He looked at me questionably as if to say, 'Don't you think I know what I'm doing?' But instead, politely replied, "There'll be no reason for that Mrs. Bell, I've been doing this for over eighteen years, and I've never been wrong. However, I will do a simple urine test in a few minutes, and you'll see the results for yourself."

He seemed concerned, "I'm feeling some trepidation from you Mrs. Bell. What's the matter?"
I did not respond.

"Lest you forget, you do have a choice and it's as simple as ABC. You can choose to have the baby or terminate the pregnancy. After all, it's not even two months, so this is the best time, especially, if you're considering an abortion."

I was not sure how relevant this would be, but I felt the need to share it with the doctor.

"Doctor, last week I had an accident at home and when I went to the emergency room, a series of x-rays were done…"
Without hesitation, he interrupted. "Last week you had x-rays done? No wonder you look so grim. It is very unsafe to have x-rays done in the early stages of a pregnancy. More often than not, the rays from the radioactivity destroys the fetus. From a medical standpoint, the most logical decision is to have an abortion. It will be great risk, if you were to have this child. Recent studies have shown that only a small percent of babies, exposed to x-rays in the early stage survive."

He was becoming frustrated, as we were hardly participating in this debate. "If nothing more, relieve yourself of the mental torture. The secretary will be delighted to schedule you for an appointment."

Larry had remained quiet through all of this, but I sensed his desire to have an input at this point. So he took the floor, "Doctor, with due respect to you if this was your wife what would you do?"

I could tell the doctor was taken aback by his brashness.
"Without a doubt, she'd have an abortion. I would want to spare her from the mental agony. But, understand this, this is your decision. Not mine! You can go ahead and solicit some other medical advice, but I bet in the long run we'll all be saying the same thing."

Larry continued, "My decision is that under no circumstances will my wife have an abortion. I'd rather have her give birth to an invalid before I allow that to happen. After all, this is a shared responsibility, and in the unlikely event that the child is abnormal, I'll be there for her and the baby till the bitter end. I'm not one of those dead-beat dads, to abort my family. Only men who cannot live up to their responsibility would commit such a crime. That's not me."

"Mrs. Bell your husband has spoken and you can go ahead and set up an appointment for a regular check up from a month from today. Have a good day."

We drove home in cold silence, because even though I preferred to have the baby,

I didn't like the feeling that I did not have a say in the matter. And I felt the old fears returning. The ensuing days were traumatic. I'd jump out of my sleep, feeling petrified. I had terrible nightmares, where I saw deformed objects resembling aliens from outer space. I still suffered intense pains from my cracked coccyx. But now that I knew I was pregnant I had to cease taking the pain suppressant. The nights were miserable. Weeks passed and I found it very difficult to cope with the situation at hand. By this time we consulted several doctors. They all recommended that I have the abortion.

I seriously considered the advice of the doctors, but I wish I had someone in whom I could confide. How I wish that Kevin lived close by so I could sit and talk with him and get his brotherly advice. He was such a good listener. I needed to unload, but there was no one. No one that I trusted!

Suspecting that I may follow through with the doctor's advice Larry made sure his threat was loud and clear.

"Nora, if you ever abort this child, you will pay with your life, because I will KILL YOU."

I knew he was serious, but at this point, I refused to tell him that I had decided to have the baby.

CHAPTER TWELVE

The season had just changed to summer, and the heat in Brooklyn was unmanageable. It was a hot and miserable Friday night, when I suddenly awoke, from the baby's tossing and kicking. I reached over to cry on Larry's shoulder, and to get a little reassurance that everything would be okay. Larry was not there. I held onto the pillow and cried. I got out of bed, turned on the light, tore off the sheet and shook it with all my might, as I refused to accept it. I started searching everywhere. I looked around the room, in the closet and in the bathrooms. I went downstairs and searched in the kitchen, the family room, and the basement yet there was no sign of Larry. I braced my back with my hands, while I slowly climbed the sixteen step stairway, from the basement to the kitchen. Then, I sat at the foot of the other set of stairs leading to the bedrooms, and with my face cupped in hands I asked, 'Where could Larry be? He's not slept out for a long time so something must be wrong. Even though he has his short comings, I can see that he's making an effort to change.' My emotions were confused, as to what direction to take, and in my perplexity I asked, 'If I were to receive news that Larry is no longer with us, would I rejoice or mourn?' Just the thought scared me, as this concern did not help my bewildered state, it only brought to focus, a very gruesome picture. The harder I tried to dismiss it, the more vivid it became that Larry was dead...

I called around to all of the neighboring hospitals and no one had any information on Larry, or anyone matching his description. I was tempted to check with the morgues, but I decided to wait for the twenty-four hours to pass. How was I supposed to tell Julius and Luther that I had reason to believe their father was dead? Julius who was observing my behavior, came up and put his hands around me, "Mommy I know you're crying for Daddy, but don't worry, he'll be home soon." I turned and hugged him and suddenly I thought, 'What if Larry is okay? Not only would I feel foolish but also disappointed.'

Because part of me hoped that all my tears and suffering were not in vain. Once again, my emotions were confused but as I glanced in the mirror, I couldn't believe my eyes! I look deranged! 'What a sight!' I thought. 'Whether Larry is alive or dead, I've got to pull myself together. The least I could do is look decent, as I expected the police to arrive any minute. I started getting ready to go to the bathroom, when the door slowly opened.

"What's going on with you?"

I realized this was no ghost. He sounded cold and sarcastic. As he continued, "Why are your eyes so swollen and red? You look terrible. Are you preparing to go to the morgue, or something?"

Wasn't that ironic, he thought I was ready for the morgue, while I thought, that's where he might have been. As he looked me up and down, he said, "This is not the type of look that will keep me home, on the contrary, it will keep me roaming the streets." I hated him!

In utter frustration, I turned to him, "Where have you been Larry? I almost had a nervous break down, contacting hospitals and police stations to see if they had any information on you."
"Nora, please! Spare me the excitement. Just be cool, and I'll explain everything in due course."

I remained quiet, as I waited for an explanation. Softly he broke the news, "I did not want to tell you this, but in the last couple of months things have gotten progressively worse in the insurance industry. I've a few hundred dollars worth of charge-backs, and for the next couple of weeks very little money will be coming in. This has created undue stress on me, especially with you being pregnant, so I decided to approach one of my clients about the situation. To my surprise, he made me an offer. His recommendation was that, I drive taxi at night, so I can at least keep food on the table. After receiving my printout yesterday, I went into a sudden state of depression, so I went straight to the taxi stand, and took him up on the offer. I drove all night and although I didn't make a killing, I managed to round up your grocery money. Here Nora, take this and see what it can do."
He removed a wad of dollar bills from his pocket, which he placed in my hand.

"I wish I had more, but don't worry better days will come. Nora I want you to understand that I love you very much and there is nothing that I wouldn't do to ensure that you and the kids are adequately provided for."

As I listened, my heart went out to him. 'At least, he's making an effort,' I believed every word he said and I hugged him, and reassured him of my love.

While he showered I made brunch, which I served him in bed. This was my gesture of appreciation, for him taking the initiative to do something, to offset the bills without my nagging. I consoled myself, 'After all, he's not that bad, just a diamond with some rough edges. I'm prepared to do some cleaning so that one day, it will be nice and smooth, and well worth the wait.'

Our relationship was back on track, until about two weeks prior to the birth of our third child. One evening, shortly after he arrived home, he commented, "It's very important that we speak this evening. There's something bothering me, and I need to get it off my chest. Why don't we go for a drive, so we can talk?"

Immediately I became alarmed, and was very eager to hear what this was all about. As we drove he started speaking, in a low, and controlled tone.

"Do you remember the night that I didn't come home? Well, I lied. My explanation was partly true. I did go to the taxi stand, but it was not to negotiate to drive one of my client's cars. It was to pick up his secretary, who I've been seeing, long before you became pregnant."

Instantaneously, my body went into shock, and I could feel myself becoming increasingly cold. He continued, "Those mornings when I'd meet you at the gate, when you were leaving for work. I was coming from, her house. After I'd recommitted my life to God I'd promised Him that I'd never be with another woman other than my wife. But that particular Friday evening the desire to sleep with her was too strong for me to fight and I gave in. Nora it's hard to play the dual role, especially with me professing Christianity but seeing I'm only human, I gave in. After making love to her all night we woke up together and went at it again. On the fourth round I glanced at my watch and when I saw the time, I quickly pulled out and told her I had to go. She started to cry and like any other man I finished up what I'd started. I grabbed my pants and quickly rushed through the doors as I couldn't take any more."

There was a long pause before he continued. "Oh by the way the misappropriation of funds should be no longer a mystery. But as I left, I became concerned as to what explanation I'd give you. So I returned to the taxi-stand and changed a $100.00 bill into singles."

I remained speechless, as he continued, "Then I volunteered to change a couple of tires, so I could get soiled and dirty, in the effort to make my story more convincing. You might not believe this, but it's only you that I love, everyone else is just a fling. Nora, women are my weakness. I want to get out of this dirty living. I want to be able to be true to you. Can you please help me by accepting my apology? Nora, please forgive me."

I was too gullible. My only concern at the time was voiced when I turned to face Larry, "So are you still going to be sleeping with her?"

CHAPTER THIRTEEN

The out of space creatures floated in the air, my baby was unidentifiable. I cried, "No, No, that's not my baby. Why God? Why?"

Someone was shaking me real hard, "Nora, it's okay, it's not real. It's a nightmare."

I opened my eyes, and Larry lay next to me stroking my brows, "You'll be just fine my darling, everything will be…"

"Lord, please, please help me, I can't bear this,"I cried.
The pain started from my abdomen, and quickly penetrated my lower body. It settled right at the base of my spinal cord, and would not move. These labor pains were much more severe than the other two put together. I tried to curl myself up in the fetal position, but my stomach was too big. Everything about this baby was so different.

As the pains intensified, I called out to God."Lord please don't punish me, I didn't have the abortion, I listened to you and I'm having this baby, so please have mercy on me."

A great deal of my suffering was mental. Fear rapidly spread to every sensory nerve, and with the excessive pains, I thought I'd die. Larry was agitated, as he couldn't understand why this was so different. In his frustration he looked at me, "You should be getting better at this, but instead you're getting worse."

I had no time for Larry. I just thought that my body was never meant to deal with this level of pain. All I wanted was for them to rush me to the delivery room, before they were forced to check me into the psychiatric ward. I bawled as the pain racked my body, and Larry was finally convinced that I needed emergency help. He called 911, and soon, I was being rushed to the hospital in an ambulance. I was examined and the doctor informed me it was false labor. They refused to admit me, despite the pains. I returned home, with my unpacked suitcase, feeling like a simpleton.

Right through the night, the pains steadily increased, the contractions were down to every ten minutes, and I was admitted at the break of dawn on July 2, 1981. In all, I was in labor for approximately thirty six hours. Beads of sweat welded on my forehead, as I bore down, yet the baby would not come. A last minute ultrasound showed that the baby was breech. With the help of God, and the direction of the doctor, the last push made me feel as though all my organs were forced out right on the delivery table. It felt like the baby was out too, because suddenly I was relieved of the heaviness. I was too scared to ask, as I knew I was about to either witness a vegetable or a miracle. Everyone remained still, and that confirmed it! No one wanted to break the news to me, that my baby was abnormal. A quick glance at Larry, and he was drying his eyes. Feebly I asked,

"Can somebody please tell me what's going on?"

The doctor stepped away, and the nurse leaned over and whispered,
"Mrs. Bell you've got a beautiful baby girl." Larry pulling himself together assured me that everything was alright.

"It's okay Honey, Lanora has arrived, and she's adorable. You can open your eyes, because God did not go back on His promise to us."

Tears of joy flowed down my cheeks.
"Is she normal? Does she have ten fingers and ten toes? Are you sure she's okay?"

"Give me a chance, and you'll soon see for yourself," the nurse replied. I cried, and cried, not for the pain I was still enduring, but for joy. When the nurse handed me my baby, I held her tenderly in my arms and blessed her.

"Lanora, you are my 'Miracle Baby,' God brought you in this world for a purpose. Because I was made to bear so many crosses with you, your middle name will be Faith. Thank God, I withstood all these tests!"

I handed her to Larry and it was his turn to bless her. After he blessed her he gave the baby to the nurse who took her to the nursery. I was still exhausted from the labor and fell into a deep sleep.

When we arrived home with Lanora, the two boys were standing at the gate like little soldiers. At the time Julius was six and Luther three, they loved their little sister. Sometimes when I had to leave the baby crying and go downstairs to prepare her formula, Julius and Luther remained in the room to comfort her. They would gently pat her back, and before long she'd lie quietly, until I returned with her bottle. Both boys were always alert and very protective of their sister.

With my two helpers, I found it easier to deal with the day-to-day challenges that I encountered.

CHAPTER FOURTEEN

It was approaching twelve weeks since I'd given birth to Lanora and I managed to put a little money aside for my overdue doctor's visit. Dr Quinone was concerned that I had not kept my six week appointment, but he learned by now that our behavior was erratic. An examination was done to ensure that everything was back to normal.

"Mrs. Bell you're pregnant again."

I was crippled by his statement. I badly wanted to dig a hole in the ground, and disappear. And never have to look in Dr. Quinone's face again. I burst into tears. Not being sure if I was seeking pity, or just disgusted with my actions.

"Dr. I'm not trying to be rude sir, but how can I possibly be pregnant when I'm still breast feeding and having my period?" I asked.

He cleared his throat before responding,
"Haven't you been sexually active?"

Not getting a response from me he continued, "Well that takes the mystery out of it. It's not a miracle. It happens. From a medical stand point I know your body needed a break, to be able to rest and regain its normal functions. But it doesn't mean that you couldn't get pregnant."

I could tell from his tone of voice that he wanted to suggest an alternative, but based on the last experience, he wouldn't dare.

He turned to Larry, who was unusually quiet, "Your wife's billing record has been brought to my attention, and from what I remember the insurance company has paid their portion of the bill in full. Mr. Bell there is still a balance of about 75% of your portion, unpaid. Now, how can we incur a new bill when the old one is not yet cleared?"

"Dr. Quinone, you have a valid concern, but please hear me out Sir. I have a plan. I'm about to start my own business. I'll be opening a martial arts school. I have the students and everything in place, so I'm ready to explode! Before you know it, I'll have the old balance paid off, and I will put a substantial amount on the new bill. I can make pre-payments, can't I?" Dr. Quinone nodded. "Good, well it's good to know I won't be penalized."

He was so smooth with his explanations. I was eager to get back to the car, so I too could learn about this new venture. We left the doctor's office and when we went in the lobby, we asked for the next appointment to be set two months from that day, so it would give us enough time to make some money. Once I reached the car I was overwhelmed with anger.

"How come I didn't know about this so called karate school of yours? You sat right in front of the doctor and not even one word that came out of your mouth was true, how do you lie so convincingly Larry?"

"Obviously you don't know who you're dealing with. This is America, and the system forces you to lie. Everyone else does, so I'm no different. Just leave me the hell alone! I've got everything under control."

I was now believing that this was his plan, to keep me home, barefoot, unemployed constantly pregnant and permanently out of shape. In the meantime, it was okay for him to have his occasional flings, to satisfy his uncontrollable desires. I was becoming very frustrated at being required to have sex especially when I didn't feel like it. I often felt like a prostitute, as Larry demanded sex morning, noon and several times at nights.

I was imprisoned! I never had my own money, because Larry controlled everything. The little he gave me was barely enough to buy baby food and diapers. If I wanted to sneak behind his back and use contraceptives without him knowing, I couldn't, because I had no money.

"If you've got everything under control how come I'm almost eight weeks pregnant, and the baby is just turning three months?" He played deaf. By then, I was boiling like hot oil. I was behaving hysterical and began to yell.

"How many times do you plan on getting me pregnant? Do you have a problem with contraceptives? Don't sit there and pretend like you don't buy condoms. Because every now and again I'll find one in your pocket and you're certainly not using them on me. Yet, you're protecting the other woman you're screwing, and preventing her from getting pregnant. But you don't give a damn about me."

I was on a rampage. "I'm going to have my tubes tied after this baby!"

"Nora you will not tie your tubes. You're too young, and this seems too final. Just trust me we will have to use the rhythm method. Plus I can always pull out on time, and that should solve it, at least for a while."

Maybe Larry thought all of this was funny, but I was the one bearing all the children.

"What we should really do, Larry, is to abstain. I've had enough sex to last a lifetime."

The look he gave me was as though I was trying to take away his life from him. "Nora you can speak for yourself, but don't try to make any decisions for me. I do believe that you can live without sex, but I can't."

"I can see why because every time we come together a new life is conceived. The minute it is born another is produced and the cycle continues. I asked you a question earlier and I guess you've forgotten, or you've chosen to ignore it. How many kids do you plan to have?"

"Well maybe this is the only thing my mother and I have in common. She wanted to have ten children but she only had six, of which one died, but her goal was to have ten kids…"

He remained quiet for a second…
"Nora, I want to have ten children."

"With whom?" I shouted angrily.

"With you of course. The last time I checked you were still my wife, aren't you?"

If I was a cursing woman, I would have told him a string of bad-words, but I choose not to lower myself to that level. But I expressed my disgust.

"Larry, let me tell you something, not even if you tie me down, no way in hell would I have ten kids. I hope to God this other baby will be a girl, so that it will balance off. Two boys and two girls, that's more than enough for me, so if this is a girl, no way will I have another child."

I knew I was in one nasty temper. Larry must have noticed this, and realized that I was in a bad mood, because he then remained silent.

By the time I got home, I regained control of myself. I attended to the children, but gave serious thought of how I'd be coping with two babies at the same time. Thinking back on the conversation with Larry, I realized that there would be no end to my dilemma. Because based on the plans he had for me, I was not even mid point of attaining his goal of having ten kids. Despite my unplanned pregnancy, I needed to get out of the house. There had to be a job some place, where I could have my children with me. I knew it would be hard to find, but I was determined to search until I found one. It was imperative that I secured this job before my pregnancy was noticed, as I had to have some sort of independence.

One day Larry's karate instructor, who lived a few doors from us, stopped by to see him. Larry was not home, so I took it upon myself to ask him if he knew of any job openings, as our situation was critical. He was very surprised. However, I informed him of our existing condition and he promised to do everything in his power to assist.

A few days later while taking Lanora for a walk, I saw him.
"Hi Nora, nice morning to take the baby out, how is she doing?"
"Just fine, but she's more than a handful." I smiled and he smiled in return.

"Hey listen, that thing we spoke about the other day, looks promising. So keep your fingers crossed, I don't want to say anything unless I have something definite to tell you. Hope for the best, and you should be hearing from me before the end of the week."

'Dear God, what if it's a situation where I cannot have the children with me, what would I do with them?' I quietly muttered.
As if reading my mind he retraced his steps, "Nora, I know you're really concerned about the children, but just in case this job comes through, there will be separate living quarters for your entire family." Immediately I became frantic, but I tried to disguise my fury.

"Okay," I replied.

As I hastened to take Lanora back in the house, I thought he might have been referring to a domestic job, where I'd be required to be servant to some rich family. That's the only way I could see us getting living quarters. I felt like going back out to the gate, and tell him that I was not interested, but I thought it inappropriate. I tried to calm myself, and look at it in a practical way.

'All that matters at this point is for me to find a job where I can earn my own money, get out of this house and take my kids with me. So if it means scrubbing the floors of someone's home, at least it's better than depending on Larry. Money is power, and if I start to earn my own money, at least I'll have more control of my life.'

One week later, Larry and I sat in the main office of a group home for emotionally disturbed girls for a job interview, which his karate instructor had arranged. The interviewer was a very strong and aggressive female. Jessica Jacobson. I admired her style. She was totally professional. I said to myself,

'One day I'd like to be like her.'

Ms. Jacobson was an assertive, articulate, well dressed, positive, self-confident female, who had direction and was in full control of her life. Her mannerism was almost intimidating, her strength remarkable, and she maintained control of the interview, despite Larry's attempts to compete with her. I knew he was impressed, but wouldn't like for me to be associated with such a forceful female figure, fearing that some of her strengths would rub off on me, and would distract me from being a dutiful wife and mother, to possibly becoming a successful career woman.

She gave us a thorough job description, and the expectations of the position.

"Mr. & Mrs. Bell, I have received some very positive reports about you both, from my good friend. The job for which you are being interviewed requires a four year college degree in psychology or social work. I'm willing to override based on the strong recommendation I received. I've also made an exception due to your extended training, working with children from various backgrounds. I was also informed that you have three children of your own; therefore you are constantly filling the parenting role, which is definitely a plus. So with your own life experiences, and your commitment to working with adolescents in helping them to develop positive self-esteem, I do believe you are prime candidates for this position.

You will be supervising fifteen teenage girls, who have been emotionally scarred at one time or another. There is a personal file for each girl. You'll be required to document the behavioral pattern and the daily progress of each one, twice daily. Mr. Bell your involvement in the martial arts will be an asset with this job, and you never know, you might have reason to apply it occasionally. You've got to be on the look out at all times, because these girls can be dangerous. Lastly the position is paying $20,000 annually per person, so you'll both be earning a combined income of $40,000. There are numerous fringe benefits, fully furnished living quarters, food, paid utilities and most importantly your children will be able to live right here with you."

With that she gave me a queer look.

"Mrs. Bell are you by any chance pregnant or plan to have any more children in the near future?"

I was caught off guard, but lied none the less. Larry must have taught me well. "Not as far as I know Ms. Jacobson, and we're not planning on extending our family any time soon."

The interview ended with Larry reciting a verbal resume of his varying accomplishments, and assuring her that we were the ideal couple for the job. Miss Jacobson tactfully informed us that there was no need for that, as we'd already secured the position. I hope Larry was exercising some listening skills.

CHAPTER FIFTEEN

The night we moved into the group home, I quietly made my way down two flights of stairs to the office, while everyone was asleep. I was very curious as to who our housemates were. Intuitively, I knew this job was no walk over then I recalled Miss Jacobson's words, 'You've got to be on the look out at all times, because these girls can be dangerous.' Each file was comprised of the mandatory daily documentation. This was the most accurate source of information on each resident that was available to us. This allowed us to become familiar with their behavioral patterns, and also gave us a history on each of the girls. We were informed that a complete record of their background had to be submitted prior to their admittance to the home. My only interest at the time was to get my hands on those records, in order to determine our safety. As I prepared to go downstairs to search the records, I asked myself, 'Is it going to be safe here?' But then I thought, 'Even if it wasn't, we couldn't go back on our word. We made a commitment to both Ms. Jacobson and Larry's instructor, so we did not have an option. Moreover, I had no intention of going back to live with my in-laws.'

Anxiously I attempted to unlock the door to the office. But I became very paranoid when I thought there was a strong possibility, that the girls could be hiding somewhere in this huge house watching me. I was nervous, but determined to open the door. After trying all thirteen keys on the ring, I turned around totally frustrated, feeling defeated. As I turned to walk away, I looked once more on the bunch of keys in my hand and decided to give it one more. The door opened on the first attempt. Easing my way in, I quietly locked the door behind me, and pulled up a chair in front of the filing cabinet. The reports varied from; house arrest, drug abuse, illicit sex and constant threats on the lives of any authority figure, mainly, supervisors. My throat was dry. So I swallowed hard as I continued my probe.

Here we were trying to re-establish confidence and self-esteem in this group of girls, whilst I was not able to unravel the complexities of my own husband. Despite my most strenuous efforts the challenges at The Home were proving unmanageable. There was also minimal cooperation from the girls and I could not continue bringing up my children in this environment. I worried for my unborn child.

Coming in late one evening, we found The Home unusually quiet. The minute we entered, we were inhaling the strong aroma of marijuana. Concerned, I took the kids upstairs to the living quarters, while Larry went to investigate what was going on. The stillness was eerie. Suddenly, Larry's voice broke the silence, shouting,
"I must get to the bottom of this, because something's wrong. This place is like a grave yard." I heard his footsteps moving along the hallway then I almost jumped out of my skin when this awful scream pierced the silence. The voice was that of a girl named Sadie, who was not fond of Larry, "Yes, I'm going to kill you tonight you ass hole."

Then I heard Gladys scream, 'Larry look out, she's coming after you.' It was as though I was hearing a karate movie from a distance. The sounds of his 'Kai's', indicated that he was defending himself against a group of emotionally disturbed adolescents. He had to physically fight off three of them. Sadie attacked him with a knife, Karen tried to burn him with a marijuana spliff and Jean rushed him head on with a pair of scissors, with the intention of gorging his eyes out. There was so much fear within me that the baby in my stomach kept leaping as if wanting to jump out. I hoped he would not be premature, but living under these conditions anything was possible.

Miraculously Larry finally overcame the revolution, and managed to calm the girls. When he came upstairs, he was dripping wet and his breathing was out of control.

"Everything's alright. I've restrained them and locked them in their rooms."

 But later when he had regained his composure, he said, "I don't think this is worth it, let's plan on getting out of here, because it's either they're going to kill me or I'll kill them one by one. It's certainly not worth spending the rest of my life in prison."

I knew he had grown to hate them and sooner or later he'd break. And these were not the kind of girls you hate. No matter what they did, they expected to be corrected with love, but never punished. They were desperate for attention and would go to any extreme to get it.

Two nights after that horrible experience, I went into labor. I was two weeks early, but I expected it. Darrel, our smallest child at birth, weighed in at six pounds eight ounces. The baby was tiny, but healthy, 'Thank God!' Once I took the baby to the Home, he had unending crying spells, so I figured that it was the environment as his behavior was vastly different from the other children. I conferred with Larry and a decision was made. We notified the management and handed in our resignation. When we informed the girls of our decision, most of them were very sad. 'No other supervisors have ever stayed this long, now what is going to happen to us?' Even though my heart went out to them, I knew my four children were my priority. I embraced the girls and said a silent prayer for them. When Gladys saw me saying my good-byes, she looked me up and down and walked away, without saying a word. I still said a prayer for her.

As we drove away from the Group Home, I wondered if one day I would understand why we had been put through that test.

CHAPTER SIXTEEN

"I hope to God, all those children don't prevent me from getting my rest in the mornings. I am an R.N., and I work the labor floor at Kings County hospital, and my rest is very important to me. Another thing, that apartment you see up there, has been vacant ever since my daughter left over six months now. My reason for mentioning that is because I'm very picky as to who I rent my place to. You folks seem like respectable people, so I hope to God my judgment is right. One more thing, I don't like to have a lot of traffic in and out of my house, I'm a very private person, and I want it to stay that way. This is where I live, and I have to protect it. One last thing, please for heaven's sake, pay me my rent on time.

I work very hard for my money, and I cannot be late with my mortgage. So I want you to know right up front that I don't deal with excuses. My tenants either pay on time, or leave. I might sound like a bitch, but truly, I'm not. All I want is for people not to use or abuse me. I left Jamaica when I was twenty-one, I'm forty nine now, and I've not stopped working since I've landed in this country. I've been a single mother for many years, and have made many sacrifices to put my two daughters through college. Because I'm too proud to get help from the government, so that's why I work so damn hard. I don't beg, borrow, or lend. So if you want us to remain on good terms, just pay me my rent on time. And by the way you can call me, Miss Bush."

As usual, Larry's voice had to be heard.

"I'm very pleased to inform you, that you've made the right decision in renting us the place, I guarantee, you'll have absolutely no regrets. As for the rent, you can save yourself the headache, we'll pay in advance most times, if that's okay with you."

"Sorry to interrupt, but I never hear people pay rent in advance before. This will be a first for me."

She didn't seem convinced. Larry regained his posture, "You see Ms. Bush we're hard working people, just like yourself, and we've always been able to stay on top of our bills. So there's nothing for you to worry about."

I too was pleased to learn this. When I realized Larry's speech was short, and to the point, I had to say something. Because I sensed her concern regarding the noise the kids were making.
"Miss Bush as it stands, I stay home with my children, so trust me, they're under proper supervision. I promise, I'll have everything under control for you."

"One last thing, and believe me I know it's none of my business, but how com' you folks can afford to have so many children, in this day and age?"

Before either of us had a chance to respond, she continued,
"Well, I guess since it's two of you, it's not so hard after all. But before you have anymore, think about their college education, it is not cheap. I'm only talking to you from experience, so don't mind me."

Shortly after we moved in, Miss Bush began nagging and complaining. I knew my kids, and they were not loud and boisterous. It was only the baby's constant crying that concerned me. Even though, I tried as hard as I could to keep them still, she insisted that they were a nuisance. The situation became very tense, but I had no alternative but to try my best to satisfy Ms. Bush. Things went as planned for the first few months, then the old financial stresses returned. By this time the little money we had managed to save, was almost depleted. Our account only had debit transactions, not once, was a credit posted to it. Shortly after, the account was closed and we were unable to pay our rent on time. In order to pay Ms. Bush, Larry had to borrow money from his mother. This only added to my stress, as I didn't see a way of repaying.

Larry was up to his usual scams again and we were on the verge of eviction. I awoke one morning and immediately rushed to the bathroom where I began vomiting. "Could I be…again?" No tears were shed. Instead, I took it calmly, and from its inception, accepted the responsibility. An abortion was not even a consideration, so I resolved to maintain a positive attitude, throughout the nine months. I repeated my affirmations each day and was committed to a healthy and stress free pregnancy.

'The life that grows within me shall develop into a positive, pleasant, caring, loving and God fearing child.'

I was determined to block any negativity that could affect the baby. It really didn't matter whether I was bearing a girl or a boy, all I asked for, was a normal and healthy child.

Being a firm believer in the 'Power of Positive Thinking,' I knew that a happy pregnancy would result in a vibrant child. So reading to the baby and falling asleep to soothing music, was all a part of the strategy. However, sharing a marriage with someone of so many different personalities did not make it easy for me. Many times Larry pushed me to the limit, but I'd quickly reflect on my decision, and regain a calm composure.

Again we were in a financial bind and seeing we had a huge balance for Dr. Quinone, we were too embarrassed to ask him to extend the credit. This left us with no alternative, than to find a new doctor. Interestingly, he was associated with two hospitals; one was the same hospital where the other children were born, and the other, a Catholic hospital. Of course, we opted for the latter, as our records were in the collections department at the other place and we didn't want to risk, being turned away.

It was challenging for me to sustain strength, as many days I became physically weak, due to poor eating habits. The food supplies dwindled, as there were no funds available, not even enough to buy groceries. Still Larry refused to take a 9-5 job. He thought that he'd not make enough money, to bring the past debts current, and provide for his family adequately. So with his negotiating skills, he convinced his family to assist him in establishing a taxi service. Once he started operations, things took a major turn, and before long, we were at least eating better, and I was able to regain my strength.

Larry became power driven, and suddenly had a desire to work around the clock. The plan was to drive taxi at night, and build a Mulit-level business during the day. This was admirable, as he had switched one of his top priorities from sleep to work. I'd prayed many years for this change, and quietly hoped it was permanent.

CHAPTER SEVENTEEN

It was winter. Each day it snowed. There was almost nine inches of snow on the ground. In the streets, long lines of cars with dead engines could be seen. Many of the trees were bent, almost touching the ground, laden with snow. Along the sidewalks, the children played and threw snowballs at each other. Luther and Julius were dressed in their coats, hats, scarves, boots, and mittens. They built a huge snowman that reminded me of Christmas. The entire city was one big white mass, and it could be easily mistaken for a cold December morning. As I tried to rub the frost from the windowsill, my fingers grew numb. I had zero tolerance for cold, and I felt as though I was trapped in an icebox. I buttoned up my robe, and put on a knitted cap and woolen socks. I looked in on Lanora as she slept, and tucked the blanket under her, ensuring more warmth. Little Darrel seemed restless, so I knew he was cold. I bent down and felt his hands and they were freezing. I reached for my blanket and tucked him in. As I straightened up, a familiar pain settled at the base of my spine.

The contractions came on suddenly, and I immediately dialed my sister-in-law. I asked her to come as quickly as possible. I called all the children and told them I was going to the hospital, and that their aunt would be caring for them in my absence. As I turned to wake Larry I felt a warmness running down my leg. I knew there was no time to waste. Thank goodness the hospital was only a few minutes away, and I made it to the delivery room, just in time. One final push and the baby was born, I smiled to myself, 'The more I do this, the better I get.'

When Patrick John entered this world, he came out with a chuckle, not a cry. He weighed seven pounds, fifteen ounces. This time Larry was not allowed to view the delivery, as this was not permitted in a Catholic Hospital. I was indeed thankful for a healthy, normal baby boy, but what would I have given to be the mother of a little girl?

When we brought the baby home everyone was happy except for Lanora. She wanted a sister, and was very disappointed. Although her brothers were always very protective of her, they hardly played with her, and she was becoming lonely. "Mommy can you please ask Jesus to give me a baby sister."

"Lanora, it's not that easy."
She seemed sad, but Luther joined in, "Mom, it must be easy for you, because every time you go to the hospital you bring back a baby. So next time, can you please bring a sister for her, because she needs someone to play with."

It was two against one, so I responded, "Well let me put it this way. If I should ever decide to have another child, I'd ask God night and day to give me a girl. That's the most I can say, I can't promise anything."

The baby's formative months were pleasant Patrick had the most winning personality one could imagine, always smiling. Darrel loved his baby brother. Many times he'd be caught tickling him, as he'd seem to get a kick out of doing this. They played a lot together, while Julius and Luther became lifetime partners. But poor Lenora, she just bounced around her brothers, not fitting in with either the older boys or the younger ones. But despite all this, the children and I were relatively happy, in spite of Larry's extra marital affairs. I closed my eyes to that reality, and concentrated on establishing strong moral values for my children.

Time went by quickly, and before long Patrick was approaching ten months. One early morning in December of 84' the phone rang at 5:00 AM. This was unusual, because it was not even daybreak. It was one of my brother's Clifford, who lived in Queens, NY. He was very low keyed and sounded sad, "Nora I have bad news."

"What's wrong? Is Mama dead?" I frightfully inquired.

"No it's Papa, he's not dead, but he had a massive stroke. He's presently in a coma in the intensive care unit, at the University Hospital."

Slowly I hung up the phone, because I could not continue the conversation. My knees gave way, and I collapsed. 'God, I beg you, please don't take Papa away. I haven't seen him in three years and I don't want him to go before I see him. Please Lord, spare him the suffering.' My pleas and cries woke up everyone. When I informed the children what had happened, they gathered around me and the bigger boys cried with me.

Larry, the 'Iron Man,' uttered, "You're all behaving as though the man is already dead, I just cannot relate to this kind of grief. As a matter of fact, all you children shut the hell up, and leave your mother alone. It's bad enough to have to listen to her babbling, plus yours. I refuse to deal with this. One thing is certain, if it was my father, I would get a hold of myself and be in control of my emotions."

I was in no mood for his logic. The man who had taught me love, and who had become my hero was dying. The pain was unbearable. During the three days that followed, I spoke to my family in Jamaica at least twice daily. All I needed to know was that Papa was improving, but that assurance was not forthcoming. In the meantime I had lost the desire for food, and overall, I had become dysfunctional.

Then Thursday morning at approximately 5:15 AM I jumped up suddenly from a dream. I dreamt I had managed to make it to Jamaica, and went to visit Papa in the hospital. When he saw me, his face lit up, becoming very alert and chirpy. He pulled me down to kiss me, then whispered in my ears. 'Nora I want you to sing to me, just like you did, when you were a child. Please sing, 'today in Glory.'

I didn't know this song, but he recited line after line, all three verses. The minute I woke up, I began to write as the words were still fresh in my mind. When I read the words of the song, without a doubt, I was sure Papa was saying his final farewell. That was the most suspenseful and unhappiest day of my life. Each time the phone rang I expected to hear the worst. This was a nerve-racking experience, and as I paced the floor I pulled my hair and prayed. "Please God don't take him away from me. Let me at least see him and sing to him before he goes."

At five thirty that evening the call came from Jamaica and when I picked up the receiver, all I could hear was bawling on the other end. Not a word was spoken. I knew Papa had died, but they were too torn with grief to convey the message. When they hung up, I dialed my brother in Queens and we went through the ritual of shedding tears. Shortly after, Janice, my eldest sister, called again from Jamaica, sounding a little more controlled. She confirmed that Papa had died at 5:15 that evening. When I inquired about Mama, she informed me that she was busy witnessing to the doctors and nurses at the hospital, about the love of God. In her exhortation she had said, 'It's a wonderful feeling to know, that my husband has left this pain and suffering to be with the Lord, where he's free from all pain. But, my question to you is, 'If you should die tonight, where would you spend eternity?'

Janice said that while she spoke to me she could see a group of people lining up for Mama to pray for them. That was my mother, a woman of remarkable strength and faith.

Memories of my father lingered on, and I could not get him out of my mind.

Despite the tears, joy filled my heart when I reflected on his love and dedication, to his family. I desperately needed someone who understood what I was going through, and would be able to comfort me, someone like an understanding husband. But, where was Larry? I had no idea where he could've been. All I had were my five children, who were mourning with me. Julius, was nine at the time, and he called around to everyone he knew, and tried hopelessly to locate his father. But, his efforts were in vain. One of Larry's sisters offered to come over and be with me, I immediately agreed, as I needed the moral support.

I was hardly communicating with anyone, but the words of my favorite song kept ringing in my ears. It was a dedication to: My Papa, my hero.
"Oh my Papa, to me he was so wonderful
Oh my Papa, to me he was so good,
No one could be more gentle more adorable
Oh my Papa, he always understood
Gone are the days, when he would take me on his knees
And with a smile, he'd change my tears to laughter…"

The following morning at about 5:30AM Larry came home. He was totally unaware of the situation. And not expecting someone else on my side of the bed, he went over to his sister in an attempt to kiss her, thinking it was me. I was wide-awake, curled up in one corner of the bed, viewing this silly episode. When he realized it was Patsy, he seemed taken aback.

"What are you doing here?"He asked.
She was shocked at his question seeing he was aware of my father's condition.
"Do you think I'm here for my health Larry? What's wrong with you man?"
"Sorry. It's Nora's father, right, he passed away?"He asked.
"Yes, he died last evening,"
He shook his head, as though he was feeling sorry about not being home.
"Gosh, this must be really hard for her, she was very close to her old man, how is she taking it?"

"Very hard. But Larry, I cannot imagine you know what she's been going through all week, and you left her all evening without even calling to find out how she's doing. Even though you're my brother you cannot detach yourself from situations like this. In her distress she tried all night to reach you, but had no idea where to start. You have to do better than this Larry, remember you have sisters."

"Patsy, check this out, it's humanly impossible for me to be in more than one bed at a time, but the truth of the mater is, I had a very busy night, busy, busy. Look I'll make this up to her. Can you help me out though? I need a small loan so I could take the baby and her to the funeral. At least that's the most I can do. But believe me, she'll get over it. Are you going to be able to lend me the money or not?"

"Larry, if it were not for this situation…You already have over eight hundred dollars for me and I'm beginning to feel that I can kiss my money good-bye. You can't continue like this man. Anyway come by the house tomorrow evening after 6:00 o'clock, and I'll have it for you."

Smiling as though he was somewhat intoxicated, he replied,
"Everyone knows you're my favorite, so don't worry, one of these days I'll make it up to you. Just remember that."

I remained quiet, listening very sadly to the continued connivance of this man. Hearing Larry reminded me how special my father had been. No way would he have left my mother, if he knew there was a remote possibility that she could lose someone as close to her as her father. No, he would ensure that he was there in the critical moments to give her the support and love she needed. I sighed, 'If only I could have a husband with some of the qualities like my father. How happy and contended my life would be.'

We traveled to Jamaica in stony silence, occasionally Patrick looked up at me with his winning smile. Many passengers on the plane admired him, and he smiled at everyone. After we landed at the airport we bumped into a lot of family members, flying in from various parts of North America, this was more like a family re-union, but unfortunately a very sad one. I was happy to see Mama. We hugged tightly and shed quiet tears.

"Nora I wish you were here to sing to your Father before he passed away."
I was shocked at her statement.
"I did Mama, but I sang to him in the spirit,"I replied.

I shared the dream I had the day Papa died. She was touched,
"Never mind my love, don't cry, feel blessed that your Father visited you in the spirit to wish you farewell before he passed. I'm sure he'd be honored if you could sing that song at the funeral."
"Mama I'm sorry, but I won't even try, because I know within my heart, that I'm not able to do it." She understood, and once more we warmly embraced.

The funeral was comprised of two services, one in the city and the other at the little church in the village where we grew up. As the hearse pulled up alongside me, I lunged forward to throw myself on the casket. When the pallbearers prepared to take it into the church, I became hysterical, demanding that the casket be opened that I could see my Papa one last time. I partially fainted, and vaguely remembered Kevin lifting me, and taking me in the church to sit with the rest of the family. Every now and again, there would be a piercing scream. Even Mama, who had been very strong up to this point, broke down.

Papa was buried in the family plot, a few chains from the house. After the funeral, family members remained in a closely-knit group, consoling each other, and giving much support and encouragement, especially to Mama.

On returning to the States, I wondered if Larry had seen, and recognized the closeness of my family. I prayed to God that he would stop telling me how much he loved me, and begin by showing me this love. Papa's death left me with a burning desire to experience a strong, true love, not just passion, but real love. After this occurrence, I decided that if I could not get this love from my husband I was not going to waste the rest of my life waiting for him to give me an emotion he did not possess. I resolved that I would be patient, and work with him on our marriage, but deep within, I was not certain that any significant changes would take place. After Papa's death I became more aware of the void in my life, and my question was; 'Would it ever be filled?'

CHAPTER EIGHTEEN

It was about six months since Papa's death and Larry tried to console me in different ways, his most accustomed being that of passion, and I often wondered, 'Couldn't he try another method, even for the sake of variation?' Gradually, I was beginning to feel like my normal self again, but, lo and behold, I was experiencing the familiar feeling,

'Dear God, am I pregnant…again?' I wondered.

I didn't want to go through the motion of hearing the doctor confirming the results, so I opted to do a home pregnancy test. As Larry and I walked back to the bathroom to take a look, the results stared us straight in the face.

My initial reaction was, 'Six children and I'm just turning twenty-eight?'

I was not amused. Larry left that day, after making several attempts to cheer me up. He realized that he was not making much progress, so I guess he thought that if nothing else worked red roses would. I felt it was a good gesture, but when I received the roses and read the card, I totally lost it!

'Nora this is to celebrate your sixth pregnancy. Congratulations. You're now more than half way to my goal!'

I could not comprehend it so I read it over and over again…Hoping that I needed to improve my literacy skills.
'My goal! His goal! Whose goal?'

Based on HIS projections, I still have four to go? So, I've now become a scoring board? Six down and four to go! This man must be crazy! Since we were playing a game, it was now between him and I, and this was one game I was going to win, if it cost me my life! Larry's plans were for me to take intermission after this game, but for me, this was the final one.

I already envisioned myself, at the finishing line, with a baby girl, and my tubes tied. It was becoming a little scary to deal with my crazy side, the part of me that would win at all cost. Being with Larry over the years, I realized if I wanted to live, I had to let this side of me die. I knew that this was the side that would have stood up to Larry and possibly killed him, for the abuse and the torture that he inflicted on my kids and I. But I suppressed it in order to protect our lives. What was frightening, I had no desire to conceal this side of me, as it related to bearing my sixth and last child. I was prepared to take control of my life and nothing was going to stop me.

If having ten children was that important to Larry, he was sleeping around enough, to pick, choose and refuse, who his babies' mothers should be. But I didn't wish to be given that privilege. However, since this decision directly related to me, I resolved to keep it to myself, and grow from my inner strength. But I didn't want to be influenced by anyone about the matter. As for Larry, he'd be the last to know. I'd remain his subservient wife, and he'd never know of my plans for the touch down.

I became frustrated with the harsh winters in New York, especially after being informed by my physician that I was anemic. I toyed with the idea of exploring the possibility of moving to a warmer state. The doctor apprised me that having the children so rapidly took a toll on my body, which resulted in a significant loss of blood. Therefore, the weakness and exhaustion at the time was understandable. During the winter, whenever I had something cold to drink, I had to sit in one position with my hands between my legs for at least an hour, without moving a muscle, in order to stay warm. It got so bad, that anyone standing next to me could hear my teeth chattering.

This situation was unbearable, so I prayed for an escape from the cold. Due to the pregnancy and my ill health, I was advised by my doctor to get away from the bitterly cold New York weather.

One evening, while sitting next to the heater, attempting to get warm, Marcia, a friend of mine who'd recently relocated to Florida called.

"Nora, you guys need to give some serious thought about moving down here. The environment is much better here to bring up the children, and the lifestyle is so different from New York. As a matter of fact, it's more like the way we were accustomed to living back home."

I could not believe the timing. "Girl, God must have had you call today, because I don't know how much more of this cold I can take."
She interrupted, "Do you want to take a guess what the temperature is down here?"

I thought for a minute, "How much? About 75 degrees?"
She bragged as she replied, "Much warmer than that. It is 89 degrees right now, and I'm on my back patio watering my plants as we speak, wearing a skimpy pair of shorts. Nora I don't mean to tease you, but what more can I tell you, for you guys to make up your minds. I promise you'll never regret it. Anyway, talk it over with the boss I know you can't make any decisions without him. But if you have to beg him, do it, because I know you'll love it here."

When Marcia hung up the phone, the picture that was left in my mind was that they were living in paradise, and the weather was similar to Jamaica. I felt that Florida was the best place on earth to raise my children and I knew getting away from the hustle and bustle of the city would do us good. All that mattered was to move to Florida. Later that day when Larry returned home, I discussed the possibility of relocating, and to my surprise he was receptive.

At the time he and I were in the process of studying to receive our Real Estate licenses. Six weeks later, we passed the exams and became licensed agents. It was agreed that I would be inactive, and Larry would keep his license active. In the meantime he became involved with a company that was selling undeveloped land in Florida. Shortly after joining the company, he became one of the top producers and qualified for a trip to Florida. There, he had an opportunity to view the place and get a feel for it. He loved it, and while there, he made contact with Marcia, and her husband. They promised Larry that they'd keep their eyes open for a good deal, and would have their real estate agent call us, when they came across one.

It was a chilly Sunday evening, when Larry answered a phone call from Betsy Gomez, of South Florida Home Finders. After introducing herself, she went on, "Your friends, Howard and Marcia, referred you to me. They've spoken so highly of you that I can hardly wait to meet you and your family. Marcia was very concerned about your wife's health, especially being pregnant with her sixth child. Please, don't think I'm becoming too personal, but I think the best thing to do at this point, is to get her out of the cold.

However my reason for calling is to tell you about the house that I've found for you. The description I'm going to give does not do justice to it, but I'll attempt it anyway. Before I begin, would it be possible to have your wife on the call also?"

"Sure, that should be no problem Ms. Gomez, she's on," Larry replied.

"Oh! Hello Mrs. Bell. It's my pleasure speaking with you. I understand you are dying to get out of the cold, well I found you the perfect house. It is located in Pembroke Pines, a small middle class town, between Miami and Ft. Lauderdale. It has four bedrooms and two bathrooms, situated on a lake, a huge family room, an eat-in-kitchen and a screened patio. There is also an intercom system through the entire house. There isn't another house in the area quite like this. The previous owner was a contractor, so he's done a lot of upgrades."

I was in awe. Larry's response caught me off guard.
"Betsy, what you just did, was to describe our dream home that I have visualized for the past three years. Any of the people in my Right Way Organization can tell you that. This is the house I've been describing, in our dream sessions. So your call is just to confirm, that the house is in fact ready. Betsy, how soon can I see it?"

She laughed. "Right now if you like," then paused for a minute, "Can you get here by tomorrow?"

I know he needed time to get his fare together, so I wasn't surprised by his response. "I already have appointments for tomorrow, but I can catch a flight, first thing Tuesday morning, and meet with you early afternoon."

She was impressed with his level of commitment.

"Mr. Bell, I know it will be a pleasure doing business with you, and I look forward to meeting you on Tuesday. See you then. Bye."
Collectively we said good-bye, and thanked her. Larry was able to get the money for the ticket from an associate. He was on the first flight leaving Newark, N.J. for Ft. Lauderdale airport, that Tuesday morning.

He loved the house. After the sales pitch from the agent he feared that if he didn't make a monetary commitment to bind it, we'd lose it! So he entered a contractual agreement, and a $1000.00 deposit was made.

When Larry returned home and gave me the news, I was annoyed.
"How on earth could you write a check on a closed account? Don't you think that Betsy is going to find out? How do you think she's going to feel about us, after

we deliberately gave her a bad check? That's destroying our reputation, before we even have a chance to build one."

"Listen Nora, I've got it all worked out. By the time she finds out, I'll have a certified check to her in the mail."

"I don't care what you say Larry, but you cannot continue doing this. It is fraudulent, and I'd like you to stop, because my name is on that check and I've got to protect my reputation."

"What I cannot seem to understand is the panic. Let me ask you this, have you ever seen me undertake something, and not follow through on it? Just name one instance. Just one instance Nora."
I did not answer but in the days that followed I gathered some boxes, and started packing as I was instructed.

One evening I overheard him on the phone to his mother,
"Mom, do you realize that one of your fondest dreams can now come true? You can actually own property in Florida, and come and go whenever you like."

It was then I realized that he was in the process of shaking her down for another loan. Since I had gotten to know his mother, it was the first time I'd seen Larry spend so much time with her, even to ensure that she was well. He spoke to her at least three times daily, and with Larry being a master in the art of persuasion, I knew before long she'd give in. In less than two weeks he received just about all his mother's life savings. Boastfully, he flaunted the check in my face.
"Didn't I tell you to leave everything to me? Just continue packing and watch me work. But I'm sure you thought I couldn't do it without you."

As I watched him prance about the living room, he informed me that he was only short a few thousand dollars.
"But that will be a breeze," he said.
'Dear God, I wonder who will be the next victim?'
The answer was soon to unfold. It would be one of his clients, an elderly nurse who was on the verge of retiring. He knocked her up for $6000, agreeing to pay her back, over six months with interest.

Even though I badly wanted to leave, I'd have preferred to put it on hold rather than purchase a house with other people's money that would never be repaid. But I had no say in the matter. Once we closed the deal in Florida, our mortgage payment would be $1048, plus utilities, food and clothes for five kids, soon to be six. Another major concern I had, was that neither of us had a job. This was frightening. Plus we had no health insurance. This was worse than any roller coaster ride, but what else could I have done? I had to ride it out, and go along with his scheme.

We left the house owing Ms. Bush two months rent. But when Larry assured her that he'd have a money order in the mail for her in two weeks, she seemed satisfied. We stopped by his mother's house to say good-bye, and I could see it was hard for her to hide the concern. She was very sad to see her grandchildren go, but there was another reason for her depressed state. Somewhere in the corner of my mind, I heard Mrs. Bell asking,
'Larry, am I ever going to see my money again?'
It was very sad. We drove off, leaving the poor lady in a daze.

CHAPTER NINETEEN

Half way through the journey we were forced to stop as something went wrong with the battery in our car. We managed to get it fixed, but as we traveled, the battery became weak again, which killed the headlights. Fortunately for us, it was full moon, and we were able to continue our journey with the aid of the moonlight.

We drove until the morning and headed directly for the real estate office, and shortly after to the title company. By 4:00 o'clock that evening, we received the keys from the agent, and unlocked the doors to our new home. It was indeed very beautiful. The kids loved it, especially the yard. There was no fence between the lake and the yard, and even though I knew the children were disciplined, I had a nagging feeling about the lake.

Everything else seemed okay, except for the fact that we had very little money and a lot of bills. Larry had the two loans outstanding to both his mother and client. I could not see a way to settle all these debts, without either of us working. It did not make sense. I held onto the little money we had, so we could at least pay the first month's mortgage.

From the very beginning things began to deteriorate and Larry was forced to start job hunting. However, he made it very clear that he was not keen on getting a regular job, especially after learning that the pay rate was much lower here, than it was in New York. After becoming frustrated with the job situation, he made the decision to become a full time encyclopedia salesman. I knew this business could generate adequate funds to meet our expenses, but it required 100% commitment. I was not convinced that Larry had the discipline. In less than a month, Larry was doing the business two to three days a week, which resulted in his inability to pay the bills.

By the time the second mortgage payment was due, we had to borrow. I was not at all surprised I expected that things would turn out that way.

'How can people expect things to miraculously fall in place, without having a sensible plan.' I wondered.

Like Larry often said, 'Don't worry God will take care of it.' If God were to take care of every little detail in our lives, then what purpose would we serve? I became very apprehensive, because I knew it was only a matter of time, before everything collapsed. I remembered a poem I was taught in elementary school.

'A man of words and not of deeds is like a garden full of weeds---'
That was Larry alright, absolutely no substance.

By this time all our bills were way past due and it was no surprise when our light, water and gas were shut off the same day. The children were upset and could not understand why we left New York; at least there, they always had light and running water. The older kids thought it was a sin for us to have another baby when we could not adequately provide for them.

I took matters in hand, and had a discussion with my doctor. He informed me that a tubal ligation could not be performed in the State of Florida without the consent of my husband. When I spoke to Larry about this, he was totally opposed to it. But regardless of how he felt my mind was made up. I had to coax him into signing the agreement and even cater to his needs and fancies, still he refused to sign. During the last couple of weeks of my pregnancy, I had a bad case of varicose veins, the worst I'd ever experienced. There were mornings I couldn't walk, and I had to wear very thick support stockings to suppress the swelling. The pains increased as the delivery date drew closer. When the contractions started they were worse than Lanora's. They were the usual intolerable labor pains, plus the veins, which felt as though they were about to pop.

I had absolutely no intentions of ever going thru this again, so I told myself that this was the last chance I had to convince Larry to sign the consent forms. Although the pains were severe I could not get side tracked from my goal.

Time was against me! 'Because if this procedure is not done now, I'll end up pregnant again, and only if I'm lucky, I might get it done with the seventh pregnancy! NO WAY!'

'Not over my dead body because there won't be a next time. I refuse for my children to become statistics! We must be able to adequately provide for them.

If I don't take control of my life now, then I'll end up with ten children. What if Larry becomes a dead beat dad and leaves, then I will end up with ten children on welfare for the rest of my life, without a future? This will not happen to me!"

It was a cool October afternoon, when I checked in to the hospital. This pregnancy was very different from the other five as this was going to be the last time I was going to a hospital to have a baby. I was on a mission and up to that point; I was uncertain how I was going to pull it off. I wasn't sure if the contractions were coming or going, as I was focusing on formulating a plan. Then the strategy was coming together like a puzzle, the clock was ticking and I had very little time to put all the pieces together. My adrenaline was flowing and I was ready! The pains intensified as they transferred me from the stretcher to the delivery table. Larry was right next to me as I cried out, "God I'd rather you take me right now, than go through this again." I bawled, hollered and screamed.

"Nora, is it really that bad?" Larry asked. I ignored his question then proceeded with my performance. "Larry, I know I'm not going to make it this time because I can't take this pain anymore."
By then I was gasping for breath as if on my deathbed.

"Can you please just go ahead and sign the form? Please Larry, Please." This seemed to have an impact on him, and with a concerned look on his face he asked, "Is it really that bad?"
I was fuming, but since that would not get me anywhere, I turned my head to the corner, and weakly I said.

"Larry, please just take care of the baby and the other kids for me."

With a sense of finality, I slowly closed my eyes. My strength could not maintain the screams, so I narrowed it down to deep groans. Internally, I remained strong, but externally, it seemed as though I was dying. He seemed worried, "Nora, if I sign the papers, would that make you feel better?"

I felt like jumping up and shouting, 'Yes it would.' But instead, I barely opened my eyes and gave him the look of death without saying a word. The document was attached to a clipboard, on my night table, just waiting to be signed. He stood there looking all confused. I continued to groan, while discreetly I viewed his actions. He picked up the form and contemplated for about five minutes then as he signed it, he muttered, "I can always change my mind later, but just in case anything happens, I don't want this on my conscience because I'd never be able to live it down."

I pretended as though I didn't hear a word. The minute he was through, he dashed out of the room, not caring if I lived or died. Well, I was going to live, and proudly give birth to my last child.

I immediately regained my strength. I was fully alert again, sat up in the bed, and rang the bell for a nurse."Nurse, please get this form out of here quick and get it to my doctor right now! Please do it quick for me, before my husband changes his mind."
She seemed totally lost.
"Don't worry, I'll explain later."I said.

I sounded demanding but I didn't care, it was more important to achieve my goal of having my tubes tied. A few minutes passed then Larry walked back into the room, shuffling through the papers on the side table.

"Where did that blasted form go so quickly, I knew that I shouldn't have signed it? This is totally against my beliefs."
Again, I played deaf. The only thing I did was close my ears to what was being said, and continued to moan and groan.

Within the next hour, I gave birth to a beautiful baby girl, weighing in at seven pounds ten ounces. I was overjoyed that Lanora's prayer was finally answered. Marcia's daughter called as I returned to my room, and excitedly asked if we could name the baby Tanya. With the written consent of my husband, the doctor performed the procedure, which finally ceased operations of Larry's reproductive machine!

I left the hospital with a feeling of accomplishment. I had won a significant victory over Larry. Instinctively, I knew a change was going to take place in my life. I was not sure what the change would be, or when it would take effect, but I felt it coming.

CHAPTER TWENTY

It was summer and Denise, my youngest sister who lived in Jamaica, came up to spend some time with us. The weather was unbearably hot, so when I was not helping out in the office, Denise, the kids and I spent a lot of time in the back yard where it was a lot cooler.

One afternoon we were totally exhausted after playing a series of games and hosing each other down, the kids pleaded, "Mommy, we're hungry, can you please order some pizza?" We took a vote, pizza or dinner. Well twelve little hands were excitedly thrust in the air shouting, "pizza."

When the order arrived, everyone ran in the house, washed their hands and rushed to the table. As I served the pizza I took a head count and noticed that someone was missing. It was little Tanya who was ten months old at the time.

I dashed out to the backyard shouting,
"Tanya, Tanya, where are you?"
There was no sign of Tanya. I ran towards the lake and there she was, her little head submerged, face down in the water, floating.

I felt a sharp, knifelike pain in my belly as I shouted,
"Lord, please save my baby."
Everyone hurried outside and began screaming.

None of us could swim. I was terrified of water, having almost drowned at twelve years of age. Julius, eleven, was moved by my outburst, and the thought of his baby sister drowning. He was motivated to action. He plunged into the water and managed to grab her. He too cried hysterically, as he was fighting against his fears, especially not knowing how to swim. When he came out of the water with

her in his arms she was listless. He cried, "Mommy take her quick, she's dying."
When I looked at my baby she had begun to turn blue with no sign of life. I knew
nothing about CPR but I knew God was still the greatest physician.

While I prayed the kids were agonizing, especially Lanora. She knelt in the grass
and prayed, "Dear Jesus, please don't take my baby sister away. She's the only
sister I've got, and you gave her to me, so please don't take her away from me."

Hurriedly I called 911 then beeped her dad. Just before the arrival of the paramedics
Tanya slowly opened her eyes, and moved her hands and feet. But she appeared
very weak. I hugged her, "Thank you Jesus for answering our prayers. Thank you
for giving Julius the courage to save his baby sister." Smiles broke through the
tears. The worst was past, and we knew our prayers had been answered.

That night when Larry came home he was upset at me as he thought I was to
be blamed for Tanya. "I don't know what you would have told me if she had
drowned."

"Well thank God she didn't Larry."

He switched gears as he had to pin something on me.

"Alright, alright..Now explain to me why you took it upon yourself to call the
bank about the mortgage. Did you ask my permission to make this call?"
"No I didn't but---"

"You messed up Nora. We could've owned this house free and clear without
paying another dime but thanks to you...

I could not believe what I was hearing...

The initial mortgage holder went out of business and our files were lost, so this
was our chance. But now that you've called, the file will be reactivated, and we'll
be receiving a certified letter stating our options. We either pay up the back
amount of close to forty two thousand dollars, or evacuate the premises.
One month from today, the house will be nailed up if we can't make the back
payments. By the way, thanks to you Nora this is as a result of your constant
nagging and bickering."

"I'm sorry it had to go this way, but sooner or later we would've been caught, and
who is to say what the consequences would be. On the other hand, it could be a
blessing in disguise, I might have saved us both from a prison sentence."

CHAPTER TWENTY-ONE

The sales award meeting was unusually large. Larry's company had organized this meeting to be an integral part of its marketing strategy. The company had initiated a sales contest, where the top sales person would win a grand prize, valued at approximately $5,000. Everyone sat on the edges of their chairs, to hear who had won. I was glad for this contest, because Larry was motivated by competition, and even if he didn't win, it would mean a lot of money to him at the rate at which he was writing policies. However I was concerned about the quality of the business he was generating. As far as Larry was concerned, as long as the applicant was breathing, he was eligible for coverage. Sad, but I felt this would have negative long-term effects.

The moment everyone had been waiting for had finally arrived. The Senior Vice President of the organization proudly announced.

Our first prize winner, is none other than the undefeated Larry Bell, who will receive two round trip tickets, including hotel, food, and ground fare to Israel."

Larry took the floor. "Folks it's been four and a half years, but the goal never left my mind. Every now and again I pull out my goals and read them through, and today I'm being offered that trip to the Holy Land. In closing I must add, be very careful what you put your mind on, because chances are, it will come true."

Larry's earning that month was in excess of six thousand dollars, so funds were available for us to move from our old home, to a rental property by the end of the fourth week. I was genuinely concerned about the charge-backs that I knew was inevitable. I did not share Larry's enthusiasm in going to Israel, since the country was going through political turmoil at the time. So, I opted not to go. Truly, I wanted to know what it felt like to have some free time to myself, where I wasn't at Larry's beck and call. I looked forward to enjoying my children, without having to explain everything I did. When he was around he demanded so much of my time that the children hardly had any quality time with me. More often than not, I thought that he needed more attention than all six children put together.

After he left there was a significant difference in the children's attitude. They were far more relaxed and clung to me like bees to honey. They yearned to be loved, without any degree of fear. I empathized with them, loving every minute, but my heart ached when I realized that it was going to end the minute Larry returned.

Despite my protestation about the cost, he called from Israel at least two and sometimes three times daily. The gist of the conversation was,
"Nora, you wouldn't believe how much I miss you. Now that I'm away, I'm realizing how much you mean to me. I just can't wait to have you. Do me a favor and get ready for my return. We'll be spending a lot of time under the covers."

I only knew too well that when he returned, the poor kids would be shunned, and he would again demand my mind, my body, and my time.

The morning after his arrival Larry was too exhausted from the combination of jet and sex lag, so he needed to sleep. He asked if I could go in, and open the office. The phones rang non-stop, most of which were personal calls for Larry. There was one particular call, I found very interesting. The caller identified herself as Mrs. Bailey. When I informed her that Larry was not in office, she was determined to locate him.

"It's imperative that I speak with him," she said.

"Well I'm sorry, Mr. Bell is not in office right now, but if you care to leave your name and number, I'll be more than happy to have him get back to you," I replied.

"There'll be no need for him to get back to me; I spoke with him everyday while he was in Israel so I know he's back. I'll just go ahead and call him at home."

She totally confused me as I could' believe what she said. 'Larry spoke to her everyday from Israel.' I was shocked! Calmly I asked, "Do you have his home number?"
"Of course I do, apparently you don't seem to know who I am."
With that she hung up the phone. I had to pull myself together, before I could even call Larry. To my surprise, the line was constantly busy. So I assumed that they were speaking. When I finally got thru to him he certainly didn't sound tired

and beat up like when I left him.

"Nora hear me out please, and do me a favor, don't question anything I ask you to do. Just do it. We can always talk about it when you get home." I didn't like what I was hearing.

"See the lady who called asking to speak to me, well she's out to make some trouble. All I want you to do, is close up the office right now and come home, I'll explain everything when you get here."

As I drove home I thought, 'I've been in the work place for awhile, and never have I seen a businessman closing down his operation, due to fear of another person. As I pulled up in the driveway I was shocked to see the regional manager's car, James Hyzer.

'For James to be here, it must be serious,' I thought. Walking up to the living room I overheard him reassuring Larry, "Listen man, if only you would give everything over to the Lord this situation will work out, because there is nothing too hard for Him."

Suddenly I was able to put things in perspective but I was not about to sit back this time believing all the lies from Larry. I did not care who he had with him in that room, I was just tired of his games. I felt rebellious, and in that instant, the submissive Nora died.

In a very sarcastic voice I interrupted, "James, let me explain something to you. It's a habit of Larry, to give everything over to the Lord, when he hurts me. But the minute he thinks I've forgiven him, he returns to his old ways. Now, what has he done this time?"

Larry looked up, "You don't have to make a mockery of me. All I was doing was protecting you from what could be a very embarrassing situation."

Naturally, I was very curious, "What exactly are you talking about Larry? Don't beat around the bush just tell me what's going on."

"All I'm asking you to do is hear me out," he said.

"Just talk!" I was becoming impatient.

"Remember my client's wedding where I was the master of ceremonies? Well at the reception I was introduced to a very good friend of the bride, a nurse. Ever since that night we've been having an affair. She has a very expensive taste, and does not get involved with anyone unless there's some monetary commitment on their part. I was made to assume her car installments and insurance each month. The payments for this month was due, when I was in Israel. And she couldn't wait for me to return so I could take care of them. So when she called this morning, and I told her that I was not able to continue, she threatened that she would come down to my office and display some of my personal belongings, to prove to you that we're having an affair. Nora, I desperately need your help and understanding at this time. I'm trying to save as much as I can for us to move into the other house, so right now I've got nothing to spare."

"What do you mean 'right now you've got nothing to spare?' You have six growing children, and you are out there spending our money on your concubine? Once again you've taken my love for granted and disrespected, both the kids and myself. This behavior has been repeated too often. I've had it with you Larry!"

With his head hanging low he broke down and cried.
"The worst thing that can possibly happen to me, is to hear my wife say that she no longer respects me. What's the sense then James? What's the sense for me to open up to her if I have to go through this type of humiliation?"

James, obviously sympathetic, turned to me.
"Nora you have to at least give him credit that he has opened up and told you the truth. Most men would deny it to their graves."

"Don't you see the only reason why I know all of this is because the woman threatened to expose everything to me if he doesn't continue to support her? He's been having this affair for over a year and I there's no way I'd have known about it. He'd have stayed with her just to satisfy his lust, and would've taken from his children, in order to maintain the relationship. How can I stay with a man like this who consistently disrespects and abuses his family?"

The atmosphere was tense and neither James or Larry said a word. So since I had the floor I was going to wash some dirty laundry in public right about now...

"James what you're not understanding is that I've gone this route several times before. My patience is running out, and I can't take this anymore."
I paused for a moment, contemplating whether or not James needed to hear more. Then I decided I was not going to hold anything back.

"We've literally lost the roof over our heads, and if you don't believe me, take a drive by here two weeks from now, and it will be like a prison cell."
"What do you mean?" He seemed puzzled.
"Well we've not paid the mortgage in almost three years and we're being evicted. Two weeks from now, every corner of this house will be boarded up," I said.

Poor James almost fell off his chair. He appeared nervous, and became flushed

in the face. Turning to Larry he said, "How can you be in financial planning, and cannot provide financial stability for your own family?"
Larry didn't answer, but he lifted his head and gave me one of his threatening looks, as if to say, 'If you say another word, you'll regret it after James leaves.'

James's face grew red with embarrassment, and he became very uncomfortable. It seemed to me that he was trying his best not to hear anymore. He couldn't deal with it, because all along he was made to believe that we were the ideal couple. I knew one of Larry's biggest regrets was bringing him in on the situation that day, but I was determined to teach my husband a lesson.

One of my first acts of rebellion was to go out the following day and have my hair, which was shoulder length, cut to the scalp. He always loved my hair long, and was shocked when he saw it short. When he asked me what was my reason for cutting it, I gave no answer. I grew tired of having to explain my actions. I yearned to be free, because I got a taste of freedom when Larry was away, and I loved it! Sometimes I felt as though I was a slave to this egotistic, manipulative male, from which I was finding it impossible to break away.

I wanted to be free but I felt that Larry was crucial to my survival. I had no source of income yet I needed to be independent! I looked forward to getting away from Larry and starting a new chapter in my life, but leaving my children with this man was out of the question.

Larry sensed a change in my attitude. And when I stood up to him he turned his rage to the children. I was being watched like a hawk. And he seemed somewhat fearful to let me out of his sight. Because of the tension that existed between us he became very rigid with the children and used every opportunity to take out his frustrations on them. One afternoon when they returned home from school, they sat in the family room watching their favorite cartoons. Larry stormed in screaming.

"Don't these blasted kids have any homework? How many times am I supposed to tell you that I don't want them watching cartoons? I'll kill each and every one of you if you don't move from this television set right now. Nora, I will not have these children defy me!"

The poor children were so intimidated that they got up and ran to their bedrooms. I stood in the kitchen watching Larry storm through the family room. He continued in his fit of rage, "The demons from the cartoons will penetrate their minds and before you know it they'll all be possessed."
Ironically the demons from the cartoons had penetrated his entire mind, body

and soul as he'd totally lost control.

He dashed in the bedroom and returned with his shot- gun while talking aloud. "If I shoot it up here, the neighbors might hear and call the cops. So what I'll do is take it in the bushes somewhere, and blow it to pieces."I became nervous and fearful and my thoughts were tormented...'If this is what happens when I rebel, it's not worth putting the children through this trauma. I might as well revert to the role of the subdued wife.'

He hauled the television in the trunk along with a sledgehammer and the shotgun. I was totally zoned out when I heard him shout...
"Get in the car Nora, you're coming with me."
I stood frozen. 'Coming where?' I wondered. Then he looked over to where I was standing,
"What's wrong? You've got a hearing problem?"
"No,"I feebly replied.
"Well just don't stand there, get your ass in the car,"he shouted.
I remained frozen.
"Nora just get your ass in the car!"

He opened the door of the car and waited until I was seated. I looked up to the bedroom window that faced the driveway where all the kids were watching. The poor souls were frightened out of their wits, crying hysterically, wondering if they'd ever see me again.

As he drove off, I was too scared to cry. I prayed and asked God not to allow Larry to kill me but to bring me back safely home to be with my children.

As I sat in the front seat next to Larry, I was sweating profusely, but I remained quiet. He drove to a rural area then came to a screeching halt. He got out of the car, opened the trunk and took out the television. He placed it on a little slope loaded the shotgun with two shells and aimed. I remained in the car horrified. The blast from the gun was so loud that my ears began ringing.

"God I'm convinced today more than ever that I'm living with a maniac. Lord please rescue me I pray. I don't know why he has brought the gun, but please intervene and take control right now. Lord I cry out to you that you'll deliver my children and I from this man's hold. I know we are your children and we need your protection Lord."

He returned to the car with a crazed look.
"You're pushing me Nora and I don't know how much more I can take. What you

put me through that morning with James, I'll never be able to live it down. He didn't need to know a damn thing. DO NOT TEST ME WOMAN!." He punched the steering wheel. All I could do was sit there, stiff as a statue, molded in fear. The rebellious spirit that I was trying so hard to portray instantly died.

The lives of my children had deteriorated to one of tension, nervousness and fear. Now they did not have the privilege of watching TV, all they had was fear of their father.

Our house was a den of oppression. Most mornings when the children left for school, their father would be sleeping. When they returned home at 2:30 PM he'd still be in pajamas lounging in the family room, sitting at the table, eating a healthy lunch, or most times, we'd be locked in our bedroom having sex.

CHAPTER TWENTY-TWO

It was spring when we moved into a beautiful, four bedroom house, in an up-scale neighborhood. The area was relatively new, and fortunately for us, the rent was only one thousand dollars per month. At last we were able to escape our old foreclosed house.

As we entered this new phase of our lives, we also found new opportunities. Larry had an association with the weight loss industry so we gradually moved away from Insurance to health and fitness. He became totally immersed in this new field. He approached Live Well, a health and fitness center and made a proposal for us to operate their juice bar. The management agreed, and within a week we were fully stocked and ready for business.

The bar had been closed for over a year, and opening it attracted a lot more people to the club, which increased its revenue significantly. Larry had higher ambitions than the juice bar, and after negotiations with the area-supervisor, he was offered the management of the entire operation. I was responsible for the running of the juice bar, while Larry was in charge of the club. We were enjoying the best of both worlds.

One evening he came to the club very excited about a professional model he'd met that day. "Nora today I met a model, Christine Bentley. She exemplifies charm and proper etiquette; she's the perfect role model for my daughters." I remained astounded as he continued.

"What really excites me is that she was trained in London! That's where she went to finishing school. I've already told her, that Lanora and Tanya will be joining her school. Please get something nice for them to wear, and have them ready to meet with her on Thursday. I'll be taking them to visit the modeling school; you don't have to be there. At least I'll get a chance to spend that 'quality time' with my girls, like you've always wanted. And by the way, I've also offered her the opportunity to work with us on some joint promotions for the center.

These promotions will help to generate more money for the club, and the juice bar will realize an immediate profit also. She'll benefit in the long run too, so it's a win, win situation."

Soon Christine's name became a household word. All I could hear about was her charming personality and manners. What really bothered me was that as far as he was concerned, this woman who he knew very little about should be the perfect role model for my daughters. I thought to myself, 'It's strange how a man is willing to trade his wife for a relative stranger overnight. Chances are, he's already sleeping with her.' I knew Larry and I were not going to get far. He did an excellent job at trampling on my self-esteem, and I knew the day would come when I would no longer tolerate it. I'm sure there is life after Larry. All I've done up to this point is settled. But I deserve better and one thing I was sure of, Larry did not deserve me.

Christine came to the club and I unimpressed with her beauty. Larry tried to entertain a conversation but I refused to participate, excusing myself and continuing about my duties.

Later that night Larry was furious, "I guess you think I'm sleeping with her, so that gives you the right to act like a bitch. You're a real bitch Nora, a real bitch." I had no intention of taking this abuse.

"Why are you taking all this so personal?"

"I know you think I'm sleeping with her but I'm not."

"Larry, you said it, not me."

It was a very hectic day for me, so I wasn't going to let him prevent me from getting my rest. Despite his threats, I pulled the cover over my head and tried to sleep. But sleep would not come. My heart was throbbing in my throat and I was fearful that if I slept, Larry would hurt me. For the greater part of the night, I lay there, tolerating his verbal abuse. It was horrible! When I got up for work, I glanced in the mirror. A wrecked haggard face stared back at me. I looked even more tired than when I went to bed. But I had to go to work. I had no choice. As I prepared to leave, Larry jumped up and grabbed my keys, "I will do the driving." He drove the three miles to the club, as though he was on a racetrack. My heart was in my mouth, and when we pulled into the parking space I was relieved.

To my surprise he parked the car and followed me inside. He was being driven by an unseen force. He began cursing me from outside and continued the abuse as we went in.

"You're nothing but a slut. Look at you; I detest the very sight of you. You think I'm going to rest up from last night? I'll not stop today until I teach you a lesson." His voice echoed through the club, as though it was piped through the P.A. system. Everyone heard what was going on. There were members already on the treadmills and stationary bikes. There were also a handful of men lifting weights. I wished the floor could have opened up and swallowed me so I'd never have to face these people again. All along they thought we were the ideal couple, and now I didn't even want to imagine what they were thinking. The members attempted to stay clear of the front desk, where all the action was taking place. I was too embarrassed.

The cursing and abject profanity was unending. I wilted and cried,
"Larry please stop I'll do anything you want me to do. Just stop. Please. I can't stand you shaming me in public like this. Please Larry I beg you. STOP!"

One by one members began to leave, I'm sure if they had a choice, they'd have left through a back door, in their attempt to escape a dangerous domestic dispute. I felt as though my character had been destroyed.

Everything seemed lost and the whole world was growing darker and darker. How I wish that the time would quickly pass so that I could put all this humiliation behind me. But time crawled. Larry did not relent. He reached the phone and dialed his attorney.
"Al, this is Larry Bell. I need for you to start my divorce proceedings immediately. I can't stand the sight of this woman. How soon can I get this over with?"

After further conversation with his attorney he hung up the phone and continued to berate me. I was pushed to my limit. I could not take anymore. I became hysterical as I tried to dial the area supervisor. When she answered not a word could come from my lips, but she heard me crying. I hung up, and immediately the phone rang. I barely managed to answer, "Health spa, may I help you." "Nora, I thought that was you. What's wrong?" As I tried to answer, total grief overwhelmed me, and I involuntarily shrieked into the receiver.

"My God! What could be so wrong? I'm coming over. If I'm not there in half an hour go ahead and leave. Whatever is the matter with you, it can't be good for business. I'll come and take over, so you can go home and sort out yourself. I can hear about it later."

"Okay," I was still crying as I answered. Sensing that the supervisor was on her way, Larry stormed out of the center, throwing a warning to me.

"I bet you'll never pull this shit on me again, you damn bitch. I swear I'll make sure of that."

As soon as he left, two of the members who were listening in to what was going on, came over to hug me, "Never mind, you shouldn't have to go through this. If I were you I'd get my kids together and get out of that man's life before he hurts you or them. Come Nora, we'll give you a ride home, and just in case you want anything call us no matter what time it is."

The drive home seemed so long, I was deathly scared to go in that house all by myself. But thank God, when we pulled up in the driveway, his car was not there. They made sure I got in safely then left. My head was pounding, and the migraine had moved down to my eyes. The pain was severe. I felt I was going insane! It was as though all my nerves were shattered. This man was bent on putting me in a straight jacket, but I would fight him till I die. I cried out to God, begging for help!

The phone rang and I answered. The supervisor was on the line. This time I was able to talk. After explaining the situation to her she replied.

"Nora, this is an official warning to you that Larry is not allowed on the premises of Live Well. If he ventures to defy our orders, he will be arrested. Don't forget my husband is a state trooper, so I've got the right match for him. Now let me tell you a little story. I had two managers who both experienced bad marriages. One decided to get out of the situation and start a new life, while the other stayed in her marriage, hoping the situation would change. Today the girl who kept hoping that her husband would change, is still recovering from gun shot wounds she received, when he tried killing her. The choice is yours, but remember whatever you do; Larry will not be permitted to come back to the health club."

My head was whirling. I had absolutely no idea what to do. I could not leave him. There was no place to go. Who in their right minds would shelter me and my six children? I'd rather die than to leave them. I was determined that whatever we did had to be done together. I explored all the options and we had no alternative but to continue living with this maniac.

CHAPTER TWENTY-THREE

Julius walked towards my room, "Mommy, Mommy where are you? Are you okay?"

On hearing his voice I rushed to the bathroom in an attempt to pull myself together, "Julius I'm fine, I'm just using the bathroom but do me a favor and pray that God will keep us safe, and that if it's His will for us to leave He will provide a place for us."
"Mommy something's wrong!"

Trying to sound composed I answered, "I know things are not right but trust me, only prayers will turn this situation around."

I unlocked the door. When I opened it, the four older children were waiting to hear what was happening. Little Darrel pulled me down to kiss me, "Mommy why are your eyes so red? You crying again Mommy?"

Lanora hugged me below my waist and in a soft voice said, "Mommy I hate to see you sad, can you promise to stop crying?"
As she spoke I tried hard to fight back the tears. Julius interrupted, "The last time I saw Mommy look like this was when Grandpa died. She took it really hard. Something must be wrong."

Luther, looking unmistakably disturbed, volunteered to pick up Patrick and Tanya from the sitter next door. He was always trying to help in his limited ways. When they returned and I saw Patrick's smile, I couldn't help but return the gesture. He greeted me, with a warm kiss and hug. Luther handed Tanya to me, and as I held her in my arms, I felt a rare joy, despite my fears. I still had reason to be happy because my six children genuinely loved and cared for me.

These children were all I had. I had no material possessions; neither car, house nor land. But I had them and they had me. How could I not love them with every fiber of my being? They were my reason for holding on, and I was not going to give in. There was no way I'd be separated from them. I prayed that I could release the feeling of being trapped. Though we were united by this strong love, we were also fearful of someone, who although so close to us, was the common foe. We needed a miracle.

This house was now another of my cells. Within its bars fear and love battled for supremacy, a fight where fear was always the victor. The house was stained with Larry's wrath, even when he wasn't home, the dread remained. When we moved into this house, Larry relented and compromised by allowing us to have a television in the family room. Wanting to spend some time alone, I suggested that the kids watch a movie, so I could have a chance to rest in my room, undisturbed.

As I wrestled with my emotions I thought I heard Larry's voice echoing through the walls of the room. I hoped it was only my imagination, because I feared facing him so soon after that morning's incident. Unfortunately it wasn't my imagination. There was Larry standing right over me. I had not heard him enter the room. Chills went through my body, and my stomach contracted as though I was going into labor. He lowered his voice and appeared very low keyed and composed. I knew I was in for trouble. He muttered something as he opened the closet. He removed his shotgun from its leather case. When I saw this I cowered into a further corner of the bed, my heart beating so hard, nearly breaking through my chest. The vibrations left me shaking, and for a moment, I thought I was having a seizure. Spastically, all the muscles in my body contracted and relaxed. Larry paced across the room and stood over me again, gun in hand. I attempted to repeat the Lord's Prayer, but I was so terrified I couldn't remember the words.

The crisis was so intense that I thought I'd be better off if he pulled the trigger and relieved me of my misery. My head felt like it was about to explode and for a split second, I thought that I was alone in this world, and there was no one who loved me.

I felt as though I had never mothered a child, never a son or a daughter, it seemed as though Larry was all I had. He was my only hope, yet he didn't love me. So I was prompted to beg him to put an end to my loneliness, to my pain, pull the trigger and end my misery. Suddenly the dark gloom that clouded my eyes miraculously changed into a bright light and I felt more sober. Then I remembered my children. I nervously raised my hands to my head and placed them both by my temple. The trembling was so intense that I had to put them behind my back and lay on them in order to keep them still. During my ordeal Larry stood there staring at me.

I quietly sobbed, 'God, God, God have mercy on me and my children.'

I began to shiver uncontrollably. My body was listless. I was crying and my head felt as if it were in a vice grip. I was fearful for my life and the lives of my children. If he planned on killing me he would have a fight. I was going to fight him despite my weakness because I had reason to live.

Darkness overshadowed the room. The spot where I laid suddenly felt warm, and I thought a fever was running though my body. As I shifted my position, I realized that the bed was wet. The air was stifling, the heat intense, and a feeling of claustrophobia permeated my being. It was then that I understood the real power of fear, the fear of the unknown. I realized that one could easily die while trying to overcome it.

Again Larry moved slowly to the closet, opened it and reached for a red metal box, where he hid his bullets. Peeping though one eye, I nervously observed him. I knew he wanted to kill someone.

My mind silenced the questions that posed threats to me and my children, because like him, I too had a plan. I was going to fight till I die, if that's what it took.

He walked over to me and with one foot on the bed he opened and loaded his gun. He planned to intimidate me until my spirit was broken. But with the angels of God around me, he was facing a losing battle. With one foot on the bed, gun in hand, contemplating what his next move should be, Larry was planning to take my life.

I prayed quietly, 'Lord can you hear me? Can you please have mercy on me and my children, on me and my children Lord, on me and my children?"

I was jarred to my senses when I heard the cold deadly voice break the silence, "So you're accusing me of sleeping with Christine Bently? You accusing me, eh?" Then Larry left the room.

The only contact I had with the children was my ongoing communication with God. I was in constant prayer for their protection. Because all during the ordeal I had not seen or spoken with them. I was too afraid to walk down the hallway to see if they were alright. They had been so quiet. Because all I could hear was the television set going.

'Were they sleeping?' I wondered.

I knew they were hungry, but even if I were able to fix a meal, they could not eat. These poor innocent souls, why did I bring them into this world to face all this?

Could they live through this fear? It was hard for me to cope, so how could I expect them to?

I tried to get out of bed, but after several attempts I fell back accepting defeat. I envisioned my children calling out to me, wanting to know if I was okay. I heard Julius's voice in the corners of my mind.

'Mommy you know we cannot come in there to you, so why don't you come out here and be with us? You've always said, 'we're all in this together,' but although we're in the same house, we're still apart.'

I made another valiant attempt as I called upon all my inner resources to fight off the crippling fear. Little by little a feeling of rejuvenation came over me, and I was finally able to get up. As I slowly walked down the hallway, I felt like a woman in her nineties. All the bones in my body ached. When I entered the family room the children were wide-awake, bracing themselves for any eventuality. They rushed to embrace me, almost knocking me over in their anxiety. Luther held my hand as I sat down on the couch. Patrick and Lanora attempted to talk to me but Julius tried to quiet them.

"Shhhhhh! Guys, please no talking." Julius placed his finger on his lips. All the other children followed him and immediately the room was still and quiet again. I quickly dried my tears with a kitchen towel close-by as I didn't want them to see me crying. I had to remain strong for them. Every time they looked off I wiped the tears. I was curious to know where Larry was. Was he asleep in the office? He'd been so quiet. Wherever he was, I wished that he would remain there, because all I wanted was for him to leave us alone.

In a split second, the house was transformed into a war zone. It sounded like Larry was leading a troop of soldiers. The screams were echoing from room to room. "Nora, Nora where the hell are you?"

I heard him opening all the closets, the bathrooms and the bedrooms as he searched for me.

"Woman you better get out from where you're hiding because I'm coming for your ass!"
We all held onto each other tightly, knowing that he'd be in the family room any minute. Even Julius seemed uneasy and uncertain as to what his father might do. I didn't have time to cry. Things were moving too fast.

When Larry burst in the family room it was as though we were having an earthquake. Things were shaking, the children were crying and I was hysterical. He held the gun poised to shoot and moved with maximum speed, as if expecting a time bomb to go off any minute and had very little time to carry out his mission. Hurriedly, he pulled the drapes and turned up the volume of the television and stereo. When he was satisfied that there was adequate noise in the room and that there could be no possible interruptions, he commenced his military tactics.

"All of you stand up!" He shouted.
I forgot how weak I'd felt. I forgot the pain and anxiety and immediately myself and my children jumped to attention.

Holding the gun firmly in his hand he stood next to me, shouting above all the noise that was already in the room.

"Your mother has accused me of sleeping with another woman. It is a lie. But tonight I'm going to put an end to all these lies, to everything, I'm going to kill you all one by one. But I'm not sure who to kill first? Should it be your mother? Should it be you Julius, being the first-born? It will take less than a minute to wipe out the rest of you. But on second thought, maybe I should get rid of Tanya since she's the baby. At least she won't have to witness the other murders. Why the hell am I so confused?"

He paused as he shouted.
"Let me go ahead and shoot your mother since she's the one responsible for all this."

He moved closer to me and held the gun to my temple. I saw my death. But standing right next to me I also saw six reasons for living, Julius, Luther, Lanora, Darrel, Patrick and Tanya.
And quietly I pleaded, 'God please don't take me away from my children. They're all I've got.' In the meantime the pleading cries of my children pierced my heart as they begged in unison. "Daddy please don't kill Mommy. Please don't kill her. Please."

While the five young children wailed, Julius stood erect without one teardrop and prayed.

"Lord please deliver my mother from the hands of my father."

I stood numb hoping that God would answer the prayers of my children. Then suddenly, I envisioned my mother on her knees praying for our protection and a supernatural strength came over me. I screamed with all my might.

"Lord if You are, who You say You are, then I ask you to deliver my children and myself from this man."

This unexpected reaction threw Larry off guard and confusion was written all over his face. For a minute he lost his balance and toppled with the gun. It seemed like it was weighing down on his shoulders. His hands collapsed as if he were carrying a ton of bricks. The gun fell and he sank to his knees and began to weep.

"No, No, No, I can't do this. I just can't do this!"

I remained in a trance, while the children huddled in a weeping mass, all with the exception of Julius who maintained a calm posture. The child remained deep in thought while looking down pitifully at his father. Larry was transformed into a remorseful heap, curled up like a fetus on the carpet.

When I finally came to my senses I thanked God for saving our lives. Hours went by before the other children calmed down. We knew that God intervened.

Julius looked at me shaking his head and said, "Mommy I knew that if the gun could carry seven bullets we'd all be dead by now. But the gun can only hold two shells at a time and if he was going to kill us it would be easier to do it all at once. That's why he was so confused. You either kill once or you don't kill at all. God was definitely on our side. But Mommy let me tell you, if Daddy doesn't get rid of the gun we should seriously find a place to move to, where we'll be safe."

I wished that Julius could understand my dilemma. I too knew that it was difficult to trust this man, yet there was nothing I could do. I reflected on the incident in New York where he tried to kill me.
'How sick.' I thought I knew it was unfair to constantly drag my children's emotions through this torture.

I turned around and looked at Larry soaked in tears, helpless and destitute. Lost! I shook my head. "God how can I possibly love my enemy?"

He looked at me with his eyeballs slowly turning over and sounding intoxicated, "Nora, Nora, please, please, I beg you to forgive me." Disgustedly, I walked away to the kitchen, and attempted to make supper for the children. After serving the meal we gave thanks and even though they were starving, they had no appetite. They left the table one by one without even taking a bite. I could not blame them, as I had no appetite either. That night before going off to sleep, they made one request, "Mommy can you please leave on the lights?"

CHAPTER TWENTY-FOUR

Larry's behavior in the weeks that followed that dreadful evening was almost childlike. He played the role of the dutiful, loving father and husband. Maybe I should have shunned him, as I had difficulty erasing the awful memories. Yet, I still felt there was room in my heart to forgive him. But the children no longer trusted him.

I was very concerned about their mental state, because ever since the incident with the gun they were afraid to sleep in the dark. Many nights they woke up crying from having frightening nightmares. I'd say a prayer asking God to help them sleep peacefully. I'd also encourage the older boys to try to forgive their father.

I reassured them of my love everyday and told them if everyone in the world turned their backs on them, they could always count on me. I promised them that if their father's sick conduct flared up again we'd have to find somewhere to live and move away from him. Once that was stated, the doubts crept in.

Frustrated with the reality, I committed to please my husband and hide any abuse or neglect from my own children, so they'd always think that things were okay. Though they meant a lot to me I'd often lie to them in order to protect their emotions, but I quietly longed for the day when I could look them in their eyes and tell them the truth. In the meantime I passed on the assurance that Mama always gave me. 'Remember, God will not give us more than we can bear.'

Larry made several attempts to mend the relationship with the children but several times when he offered to take them to the park, they'd ask me to come along. I knew their healing was not going to be an overnight process, but I felt confident that things would improve if Larry consistently displayed a positive behavior. He tried hard to act the role of a caring parent and it seemed as though he was really sorry for his actions.

Emotionally the children were doing a lot better so Larry and I agreed that it was time for me to return to work. After a meeting with my supervisor, she agreed that I should resume my role as manager of the health club. We decided to close the juice bar so I could be more focused and be more productive in generating sales. I always kept my goals in focus and my motto was, 'Goals were made to be broken,' so I exceeded the sales goals month after month.

It was a good feeling to know that I could do things for myself and that I could actually strategize and exceed my sales goals. I had this feeling of independence, especially not wearing the title, 'Head of household,' but having the income as 'Head.' Despite the facts, Larry still maintained control of everything including the disbursement of my check. At that time he was freelancing, merely making a financial contribution to the family. In addition, he'd slowly returned to his old habits, the womanizing and the abuse.

I'd sit back and wonder why things turned out the way they did and often wondered if I was being prepared for the 'single parent role.'

'You could manage if you had to raise these kids on your own, because you have the discipline to work and pay your bills, plus the kids would get the love and nurturing they need.'

These were just a few of the thoughts that occupied my mind. Honestly, I was afraid of failing as a single parent as I would not be able to live down Larry's ridicule. So the easiest way out was to dismiss the thought and accept my conditions the way they were.

I tried to maintain a positive outlook on life by reading books and listening to audiotapes of stories from people who overcame major setbacks. I was thankful to God everyday for life, health, strength, a job, food to eat and a place to live. I thanked God for my children and prayed for wisdom and understanding in raising them.

CHAPTER TWENTY-FIVE

Some time went by and there was no change in Larry. I grew tired of the disrespect and his extra marital relationships. I was disgusted with his sexual demands and the abuse of my children. I lost respect for him because of his inability to provide for his family. I was embarrassed when he'd use the children and I to con hardworking people out of their money. I detested his laziness and his desire to get rich quick. Larry was blessed with the gift of gab but he had no ambition.

The insignificant things he'd mercilessly beat my children for, was the one thing that I knew would ultimately drive me to leave him. I had gained strength over the years and felt like I was ready to take on the role of being a single mom.

It was the eve of my thirty-third birthday and I was having difficulty falling asleep. I tossed and turned and was very restless, I closed my eyes hoping that sleep would come, but it did not. I began to reflect on my life and suddenly the wasted years with Larry, was fresh in my mind.

It had been fourteen years with Larry and I felt as though I'd served a prison sentence, which I felt was coming to an end. I laid in a daze and wondered, 'Who's coming to bail me? Who's going to post my bond?'

There were no answers to my questions, but one thing was for sure even if no one came to my rescue I knew the final decision in becoming free was entirely up to me.

Shortly after midnight, I got out of bed I went to the bathroom and took a long look in the mirror. What I saw was my reflection, not Larry's. Yet I had allowed him to dominate me over a decade of my life. Staring in the mirror I continued to search.

'Where's Nora?' I asked. 'How could I give Larry the right to control my life like this?'

Looking back over the years, Larry controlled where I worked and for how long. He controlled my dress and the type of clothes I wore. He controlled my choice of friends and my phone calls. He controlled how often I had sex and where. He even tried to control how many kids I should have and I had to fight him to the end to stop at six.

'Dear God how can I get rid of this man?' I asked.

I walked over to the bed and gazed at him while he slept. My piercing stare must have awakened him and he jumped up.

"Have I done something wrong?" He innocently asked.
"No, I only need to talk to you." I curtly replied.

"You want to talk to me at this time of the night Nora, what could be so important." He asked.

I swallowed and pulled on my inner strength in order to address Larry.

"Larry today I'm thirty three years old, and---"

Immediately he interrupted.
"Is this what this is all about? I didn't forget---"

It was my time to stop him.

"Listen Larry, this is not about my birthday, it's about mine and my children's future. I refuse to continue living like this."

He braced himself then sat up in the bed.

"So----"

"Let me finish what I have to say then you can speak." I was shocked by my response, but I was not going to back off.

"Today I'm thirty-three years old and I have decided to take full control of my life starting now. Larry you and I know that in the past you've made all my decisions. I'm over it Larry. I can't take this imprisonment any longer, I want my freedom and if you continue to control me I will take my kids and leave. I'd rather live under a bridge with my children in peace, than to continue living a life of lies and pretence with you. I can't speak for you, but my children mean a lot to me and I'm not going to sit back and watch you destroy them.

I believe they should be a part of an environment that teaches and practices love. So the choice is yours. Are you going to support me in my effort to provide a normal and happy lifestyle for our children? Or, are you going to fight me on this? We must effect a positive change and if that's not possible.
Please, leave us alone and let us go in peace."

Larry sat there speechless. He looked like he was waking up out of a coma. His demeanor was one of shame and concern, but that was one sure way to get me feeling sorry for him, but not this time. The old Nora would have, but the rude awakening at thirty-three brought my focus on my children and left me with a burning desire to rid myself of this man.

He sat there staring me down, so I looked at him and asked,
"So do you have something to say?"

"Well it seems like you've been under someone's tutoring, but I hope for your sake you know what you're doing." He replied.

"And what is that suppose to mean? I see you're still trying the intimidation game. Please give it up Larry, that's getting kind'a old. I'm not going to fall for this crap anymore."

"Listen to me Nora, NEVER have I once tried to control you---"

"Hold it Larry, let me have a good laugh before you continue."

He was annoyed. "And you think this is funny, just be quiet and let me finish talking."

I continued to listen, "You're such a dictator, but go ahead and say what you have to say because it won't be long before I'm out of your regime."

"I can see you like to bring attention to yourself, but as I was saying I never tried to control you. All I did over the years was to protect you. But let me remind you Nora, whatever you try to change at this time will have an effect on our relationship. So you better know what you're doing as you will have to deal with the repercussions."

I guess he didn't hear the part about the children and I leaving.

'What a fool' I thought. 'I guess he was so caught up in his world that he didn't realize that it was crumbling around him.'

I felt better facing Larry and laying my cards on the table. That day he appeared subdued but I was totally unconcerned. Truthfully, I didn't care because all that mattered at this point was our freedom.

That night when he got dressed and left I felt relieved. I was no longer disappointed that I was left alone on my birthday.

Minutes after Larry left the phone rang.

"Hello"

"Happy birthday Nora!"

I didn't recognize the woman's voice on the other end of the phone.

"Who is this?" I asked.

"Nora...after all these years?"

Then I realized it was an old friend Jane McCoy

"Jane, long time girl!"

We spoke on the phone for over an hour and to my surprise she now lived minutes from my home. This was a pleasant surprise for my thirty-third.

After the phone call ended the children flooded into the room. My children got together and made up their own little gifts. They took six sheets of colored paper, put two holes at the end and tied it with a string of ribbon. Darrel drew a picture of the six of them and me, with the sun shining brightly down on us. I couldn't believe my eyes. Little Darrel's artwork was going to keep my dream alive until it became a reality. My eyes were filled with tears of joy because I knew it was only a matter of time.

"You like it Mommy?" I was so caught up with the drawing that I didn't realize Darrel was trying to get my attention. "I love it honey. But I can't believe you draw so well." I replied.

"Guy's I thank you from the bottom of my heart because this little card is what I needed to help me make the big decision. We're going to need to do a lot of praying and it might not happen tomorrow or next week, but God knows I believe it's coming soon. Just keep praying for our safety and for God to make a way of escape.

Luther expressed his conviction. "Trust me Mom, He will."

We held hands said a prayer and I tucked them in two by two. I slowly closed the door of the girls room then quietly walked away with my prized possession, my birthday card from my six hearts.

Suddenly I was attacked. "So you thought you were going to get away without your kisses."

Julius laughed as he commenced the ritual. Luther tickled me until I dropped on the floor when the smaller kids took over and started popping kisses. I was laughing uncontrollably and was not sure who was counting but up to that point they were way past thirty-three.

"Hold up guys, don't make me older than I really am."
They got up one by one and ran off to their bedrooms saying,
"Goodnight Mommy, we love you."

CHAPTER TWENTY-SIX

I went to my room filled with joy and happiness knowing that the love from my children would always sustain me. I also knew that they were counting on me to lead the way of escape. The doubts kept barging in, but I was adamant to shut them out. How could I disappoint my children when they'd put so much faith in me? I was not going to let them down and with the help of God I was going to formulate a plan.

My thoughts were interrupted by the phone. I glanced at the clock and it was eleven fifty five.

"Hello."I said.

"I won't be coming home tonight. It's raining very hard and you know I can't see to drive at night. So I guess I'll see you in the morning."

"Okay Larry."

No questions were asked as I didn't care. I hoped he'd stayed wherever he was for good. I was about to hang up, when he asked.

"By the way is it raining down there?"

"Strangely enough it's not."I answered.

"So you don't believe me, right? I can always put someone who can verify that it's raining here."

"You don't have to because I don't care."I answered abruptly.

I hung up the phone and had a good night's rest.

The next day when he came home he informed me that he was moving out for a few months so he could decide what he wanted to do with his life. Several questions crossed my mind. At thirty-eight years old, married with six kids shouldn't he have thought about this before? Or maybe he could find a woman who'd be willing to work during the day and to support him while he slept. His contribution to the relationship would be to provide 'Sex on demand.'

'What an idiot!' I thought.

Larry was surprised to see that I was not putting up a fight or questioning his decision. The only concern I had was to get financial assistance for the children.

As if reading my mind he said, "Don't worry I'll take care of my responsibilities, I'll be functioning with a clearer head so money won't be an issue."

"I hope you'll live up to your word." I said.

He gathered most of his belongings while muttering something under his breath. Larry left without saying goodbye to the children.

After Larry left I had time to think. 'My priority must be the children because now that Larry's gone I have the opportunity to bond with each of them. I'm the only person they can turn to because they're very distrustful. I'll spend my time loving them like my mother and father loved me.'
There was a loud knock at the door. For a minute I thought Larry changed his mind and returned home. I couldn't hide the disappointment as I opened the door.

"Don't try to tell me you're missing Larry?" Kevin's question was sarcastic. I quickly helped him with a bag he carried.

"Oh that's just a little lunch for you and the kids."

"Thanks Kevin, but the reason I was looking sad is because I thought Larry changed his mind."

"Well that makes me feel better. Nora, I know it's going to be hard but Larry was more a liability than an asset. Like Mama always say 'God will not give you more than you can bear.' A concerned look came across his face. Speaking of Mama, "Janice called and told me that she has taken a turn for the worse. She's losing her speech, so keep in mind we might have to go to Jamaica soon."

"Dear God I couldn't take anything happening to Mama now Kevin, I'm going through enough as it is."

"I just wanted to keep you posted but despite everything you have reason to celebrate because the 'Old fart' is finally gone."

We smiled and embraced each other.

Over the next few weeks I'd stop by Larry's office to drop off bills or occasionally pick up a little money for the kids. Many times he remarked how well I dressed but one day he mustered up the courage to ask.

"Nora how is it that lately you've been looking so good you never dressed like this before. Lately I've noticed that your appearance has taken on a new form. It's not that I don't like the change. What I don't understand is the reason for the change, therefore I'm left to imagine anything that comes to mind." I simply smiled. "I can understand how you feel," and left his office.

CHAPTER TWENTY-SEVEN

It was early September when my older sister, Janice, called to inform me that Mama was rapidly deteriorating. She was unable to control her bladder or her bowels and lost her ability to speak. I knew she wanted to say goodbye and it was important for me to support her in her final days.

I arranged for Jane's cousin to stay with the children as Larry had already left the house and abandoned his responsibilities. I informed Larry of my plans to travel to Jamaica. We parted coldly, both of us knowing that there was nothing left of the relationship.

When I arrived in Jamaica and saw my mother I almost collapsed. All the bones in her body were clearly defined as she only weighed eighty pounds. Nothing about her looked the same. But the person on the bed was in a transitional phase, preparing to leave this world and assume a new body. All my siblings surrounded the bed. We cried and prayed through the night. The next morning, however, she died.

When I could not contact Larry I called Jane and asked her to convey the news to him. When he returned my call his response was cold and nonchalant.

"I'm sorry to hear about your Mother's death, but how does that affect your plans of returning home?"

"Did I make a plan with you Larry? Anyway, all I'm doing is informing you that I'll not be returning until after the burial."

He began to rant and rave. "What's going to happen to the business? Damn, I need you here."

That was it. This man had no compassion. I was angry and I yelled in the receiver.

"Larry take your business and shove it …

"Listen to yourself. I've never heard you speak like this before, and you call yourself a mother. Tell me what type of mother are you anyway?"

Without responding to his question, I said. "Do me one favor. Since I'll not be returning soon, please go to the house and stay with the children. Jane's niece can only stay for a week. At least you'll have an opportunity to spend time with them."

The time went by quickly and I returned to Florida after the burial. I went through immigration fairly smoothly, and as I entered the waiting area I saw Larry and the kids. I took a deep breath, 'Lord how am I supposed to greet this man?'

I decided to go with the flow, so I walked up to him and barely brushed a kiss on his cheek then went on to warmly embracing the kids. I was conscious of his stare then he remarked, "That was some kind of greeting Nora, might as well you didn't do anything."

I never answered but focused my attention on the children.

We got in the car and Larry started out with what he referred to as good news. "Nora, I've made some changes and I hope you're excited about them as I am."

"What are they?" I questioned.

"Well I've returned home for good." He quickly looked at my reaction and I didn't have to say a word.

My heart sank to my belly, as this was not what I wanted to hear. He wore a look of frustration as he spoke. "Can I ever do anything right for you? Here I am thinking I was doing something good by moving back home so I can at least save my marriage, and look at you. Disappointed!"

"Don't you think it's a little too late to try?" I asked sarcastically.

As I entered the house I could see that he made a great effort in putting the place together. The house was taintless. There was a vase with freshly cut sunflowers sitting on the coffee table, with a card from Larry expressing his love for me.

He was extremely calm over dinner but towards the end of the meal I finally broke the silence.

"Larry, I have a letter I'd like you to read after dinner."

"No give it to me right now." He replied.

I looked up at him. "Okay."

While Larry read the letter, I learned that he'd searched all my personal belongings trying to glean some information as to my whereabouts while I was away. Jane's niece told me that he'd even searched the garbage attempting to find clues of my unfaithfulness. When I heard this, I knew I had done the right thing in writing the letter.

When he was through reading it, he turned to me and said,
"I suppose you received directives from your family to write this letter."

I smiled at his implication.
"Larry, this is about you, me and our children, no one else. My family had nothing to do with this. The letter was only an informational piece, so that you know where I stand. However, if there isn't a positive change in your behavior towards us, you might as well start packing for good. We'll be better off apart and a divorce will be inevitable."

His mouth dropped open when he heard me speak. The side of his mouth was twitching from nervousness.
"Nora, is that what you want?"

"It's not about me anymore, it's about my children. They don't deserve to continue living in fear. Right now I'm only prepared to do what's in their best interest."

He tried hard to conceal his shock. "After reading your letter, I will never trust another woman. I cannot bring myself to believe that you married me out of pity. All these years I thought I was your very breath but tonight I know that you are the master of deception. But you've taught me a lesson, which I'll take to my grave. As long as I live I'll never trust another woman, you're a bunch of traitors make belief is your game and all you do is break a man's heart.

I do not accept any part of your letter. It's a curse and the only thing to do is for me to burn it. You'll not impact my life in a negative way Nora, I'll not let it happen. Just stand back and watch me. I promise you'll regret every negative thing you've ever said about me." He hastened to the back yard, lit a fire and in no time my letter became ashes.

Even though he burnt the letter, chances are he committed the entire content to memory. So I sensed that he felt he was at risk of losing me. Like some men Larry thought that he could buy me happiness. But little did he know that happiness was not in the things he bought me, but in his behavior towards me. In the upcoming days he bought me jewelry and designer clothes but none of that mattered anymore.

CHAPTER TWENTY-EIGHT

The following Friday evening after cleaning the house and feeding the kids, Jane and I went to visit Kevin. We were playing scrabble for the most part of the evening so I arrived home about 10:00 PM. I found it strange that the children were not home.

'They had to be out with Larry.' I thought. 'Even more reason to be concerned.' The side door which was normally left unlocked was secured. I didn't take my keys as I'd expected for the children to have been home. So Jane was kind enough to offer to wait with me until they arrived.

We waited for about thirty-five minutes before they came home. One glance at Larry and I knew something was wrong. I immediately said goodnight to Jane and followed them inside. My children were shaken with fear. They were confused and frightened as to how to deal with the pressure from their father. I was curious to know what transpired when they were out. As I observed, I was able to sense the pain and torture that was inflicted on them. I quietly vowed that I'd come to their rescue and when the time was right, I'd run away with them never to look back on Larry.

Larry assumed the role of an army officer and demanded that we meet in the dining room for an emergency meeting. The kids and I sat humbly, as our fate was in the hands of this mad man. He was filled with arrogance as he spoke.

"Nora, you're an evil woman and I must get away from you."
He punched the table as he continued to express his anger.

"And I need a divorce from you NOW!"
He said the word 'NOW' so loud that we could hear it echoing in the house.

Initially, I felt like laughing in his face, as he was not making any sense. But I was not interested in the trivialities. My focus was more on my children.

"What have I done now?" I asked.

"You're destroying me before my children; Julius said you're trying hard to turn him against me." Larry was lying through his teeth; he couldn't even look me in the face while he spoke.

This was the last thing I expected to hear. But Larry had the ability to twist and turn things in order to make his story believable. I took a quick glimpse at Julius and tears were rolling down his cheeks. The poor child could not say a word in his defense. Of course, Larry didn't want him to mess things up, so he ordered him to his office.

The minute he closed the office door, Luther told me the entire story in record time. They'd grown accustomed to passing on information quickly without getting caught. So he spoke very quickly, as he didn't know how much time he had.

"Mommy, Daddy was very upset when he came home and didn't see you and he started to ask us a lot of different questions. When we were not sure of the right answers he forced us to get in the car. He drove out really fast and said that if he didn't get his answers he'd crash the car and kill all of us.

He made Julius sit next to him and was always shouting at him. Mommy this is what he said to Julius, 'Wouldn't you say your mother is turning you kids against me?' Julius told him no.

That was not what he wanted to hear so he continued to scream.
'I know you're covering up for your mother, but to prove you're lying, she even came to me the other day and told me about the incident with you.'

This was really hard for Julius Mommy, because he didn't know what to say.

'Now let me hear your side of the story and you'd better come straight because it would be no sweat off my back for your mother to hear about you all on this evening's news.'

Mommy, all of us were crying because he was driving really fast. He started to swerve the car off the road to scare us some more. I hope you were there so you could pray that he wouldn't crash the car and kill us. But I was praying the whole time in the back seat."

I couldn't fight back the tears, thinking that I shouldn't have gone to Kevin's.

"Mommy, Julius was sweating like crazy as he didn't want to say the wrong thing, so he started to cry. Daddy stopped the car in the middle of nowhere, opened the door and pulled Julius out. He picked him up, shaking him like a rag doll and Julius began screaming.

Mommy I've never seen anyone sweat as much as Julius did, you couldn't tell the sweat from the tears. When Daddy was done scaring him to death he shoved him back in the front seat and said.

"I'll finish up with you when we get home. I don't think you kids are aware of the fact that your mother is having an affair. Of late she spends a lot of time away from you all, so that's a clear indication that she's tired of being a mother and is ready to go roam the streets. He cleared his throat then glanced in the rear view mirror.
'Now Luther it's your turn.'

At the time I was still praying for Julius but then I realized that I had to start praying for myself.

'What time did your Mother leave?'
She left here around 6:30 Daddy.

'Who did she leave with?'
She left with Aunt Jane, Daddy.

'Was she dressed like she was going out?'
I don't remember what she was wearing, but maybe Lanora does, Daddy.

So turning to Lanora he said.
'So tell me Lanora, what was your mother wearing when she left this evening?
'She was wearing her orange shorts set and her white slippers Daddy.'

'Very Good.'
So he started up with Julius again.

'Julius one more thing, did your mother say where she was going?'
'Yes Daddy. She was going over Uncle Kevin's.'

'It's interesting how she spends so much time at her damn brother's house.'
Mommy I started praying for Julius all over again because Daddy picked on him

more than the rest of us, since he was the oldest one.
'So Julius, do you think that your Mother cares for me?'

He did not know how to answer this one, so he asked Daddy a question.

'Do you mean if Mommy loves you?'
'Precisely.'
'I know she does Daddy, because she always goes out of her way to---'
He didn't get a chance to finish because Daddy was screaming at him again.

'What do you mean 'Go out of her way?' She doesn't go out of her way to do a damn thing. This is her duty. So you had better watch your choice of words boy.'

When he pulled up in the driveway and saw Aunt Jane's car he said.
'Now this confirms everything, Jane is the one who's trying to break up my marriage.'

Luther could not say another word as his father shoved Julius out of the office. The poor child was a nervous wreck and was crying uncontrollably.

Larry shouted as he held him by the back of his neck.
"What are you crying about you faggot! I'm ashamed you're my son I know you're covering up for that bitch and if I find out I'll kill you in your sleep…Now shut the hell up and try to focus like I told you to!"

I knew he spent the last half hour programming Julius, so the child had no choice but to carry out his commands.

So once again, he resumed his position at the head of the table, more confident than before.

"So Nora, the puzzle is slowly coming together, you no longer have to come to me for anything because you now have a man in your life. Everyday you get all dressed up, pretending you're going to your blasted brother, and you think I believe that? But trust me, I'll fix your ass tonight, and when I'm through with you, you'll agree that a woman's place is right here in the home. And on top of that your eldest son has spoken. It's a shame I wasn't aware of this before. You're a piece of shit and you're a poor excuse for a mother. You must be whoring down the streets why you're never home. What type of example are you setting for your girls? You bitch, you make my stomach turn. I'm telling you one thing if you keep this up, you'll end up dead. I want a divorce and I'm going to fight for custody of my six children. Because there's no man alive who'll take you up with six kids. So

I'll take care of them while you whore down the streets."
I became pale, and my lips turned blue, because all I heard from what Larry said was about him fighting for custody of my children.

'Not my children,' I thought. 'I'd die before that happens.' I consoled myself.

But his rage continued, "What these kids need is a real parent, someone who's always there for them, not someone who's constantly roaming the streets at night. And I know you must agree that they're much better off with me. So why don't you go back to where you were and leave myself and my kids in peace?"
The children were hysterical because the last thing they wanted was to be left with their dad. But when I saw Julius crying uncontrollably again I knew the situation had become unbearable. The poor child felt partially responsible for his father's actions.

Larry dismissed the children from the meeting and sent them to their rooms. As they left they turned around, looking back at me as if to ask, 'Mommy are you going to be okay?'

Recognizing their concern I said. "You guys make sure you say your prayers before going to bed"

They read between the lines, but it did not stop the tears. Larry had no concern about the emotional state of the children he was going crazy trying to find something to pin on me.

Turning to me he said, "You're playing with my emotions, aren't you? I don't think you realize what you're doing to me, because I'm about to break"

He looked me in the eyes as he spoke. Fear gripped me, as I had no clue what he'd do next. He sat staring into the open space as though he was losing his mind. To my relief, he stormed in the bathroom, washed his face, changed into a black suit and white shirt and left through the front door. At approximately 11 PM, he left the house, fully dressed like a company executive. When he slammed the door behind him, I prayed that he'd drop dead and never return. Larry's plan to fight for custody of the kids was not because he loved them or wanted the best for them. His was a game of manipulation and power, and with those ground rules I would not even compete.

For me, my children's lives were precious; they were priceless and there were no games involved. My only interest was for the children to be with the parent who could offer them a more stable and solid foundation. One that conformed to biblical principles, one that would focus on a healing process for their torn emotions, one that promoted high standards and a commitment to education and one that taught the importance of loving and respecting one another.

I was not going to give in to Larry. So with my renewed commitment I walked down the hallway to check on the children. They slept in pairs and as I looked on their tear stained faces my heart broke as I cried out to God. "Why God? Why did I bring them into this world to face such peril?"

They were restless and I felt guilty for constantly seeing them go through the frequent bouts of fear. I was afraid that this could have lasting, negative repercussions on them. But despite the turmoil, I knew God was going to deliver us.

That night I refused to go to my bedroom, as I felt the urge to be close to my children. I made my bed on the sofa in the family room. It was uncomfortable, but I decided to sleep there. I dozed off intermittently, as I tried to plan an escape.

Suddenly the front door burst open and I was jarred to my senses. When I saw Larry my heart was in my mouth, my tongue became heavy, and I was lost for words. Every pulse was throbbing. When Larry left the house earlier that night, he was dressed in a suit. But now, he wore a black and red karate uniform, a red band was tied around his head, his feet were bare and he had his sword tucked by his side in his black belt. I knew beyond a shadow of a doubt, that I'd fallen off to sleep again and I was still dreaming. But when I heard Larry scream 'Kai,' I knew my time had come!

Within seconds I was drenched in cold sweat. I couldn't think straight. The fear was back! He took another step towards me, shouting another loud 'Kai.' With that he pulled out his sword and held it above his head. He removed the top of his karate uniform and knelt in front of me, with the sword pointed towards his stomach. He spoke in a trance-like voice.
"Nora, do you know what Hara-kiri is?"

I could barely manage to reply,
"No."

"Well what I'm going to do tonight is kill you then take my own life. But first you must know how much I love you."

I attempted to look in his eyes, but his stare was too deadly. All I wanted to do was live, and hold onto my sanity.

Continuing to kneel he said, "Nora. I'd rather kill you than let someone else have you, and enjoy the pleasure you give. You belong to me and I resent the very thought of sharing you. I love you too much."

He paused for a quick second then continued.
"You think I'm joking, don't you?"

I couldn't speak.

"Well, watch this—"
He remained silent for awhile then crouched and began to breathe heavily. The breathing became increasingly louder as he went off into some type of deep meditation. He began chanting and cutting his body with the tip of the sword. As the blood seeped though the wounds, he told me that he was proving the depth of his love for me.

"What I'm about to do is write your initials right against my heart. That's where you belong and no one can ever take you away from me."

He used the tip of the sword to scratch my initials on his chest. I was too scared to even move an inch, as I realized that I was dealing with a real psychopath. I cried out to God. Something over-powered me, and I let out a piercing scream, which unwittingly broke his concentration and woke Luther. He came running towards me, barged into his father and began wrestling with him to drop the sword.

Larry had trained all the boys in martial arts and Luther was extremely focused on the techniques as he'd practiced a lot with Julius.

When Larry realized that his plans had been interrupted by a child, he pushed him aside saying, "Boy, I'm the master and you're the student, and you never ever pull that on a higher rank. You could've lost your life."

Luther was determined to save my life and continued to wrestle with his father until he succeeded in getting him to drop the sword. As was expected, Larry went through the usual transformation from being haughty and powerful to a meek, harmless soul. With some sort of concern in his voice he suggested that I call the police for my own good.

"I'm sure you'll feel a lot safer with them here."

He handed me the portable phone and as soon as I was about to call 911, he snatched it from my hand and threw it to the floor.

My concentration was broken by Larry's disgusting plea.
"Nora, do we have any rope in the garage?"

I did not reply.

He went out to the garage, and I could hear him rummaging for something. I hoped he found what he was looking for and would leave us alone. By this time all the children were awake, and huddled around me. He returned from the garage with a rope. His voice was broken as he spoke.

"When you guys wake up tomorrow morning, you'll find my body hanging from that huge tree in the front yard."

No emotions were shown, no attempts to dissuade him. In fact we all hoped that he'd carry out his plan. Feeling dejected he continued.
"I just thought I'd warn you so you'd be prepared to deal with the trauma."

He left, and more than ever, I wished that he'd carry out his threat. If I had a say in the matter, I'd have preferred if he didn't choose to hang himself from the tree in my front yard. Florida was filled with trees and he had a lot to choose from.

I didn't hear from Larry in two days and I was beginning to think that he actually did it. Later that night, however, the phone rang at about 3:30 in the morning. It was Larry threatening me.
"Nora, when I get home you'll be a dead mother." He hung up the phone. I ran to the kids' room.

"We have five minutes to leave the house. Let's get out of here before your father comes----."
We only had time to find a place of refuge.

As I turned the corner from the house, I heard Larry pulling up to a screeching halt in the driveway. It was that close! I stepped on the gas pedal and drove like a manic to Jane's house. When we got there, we ran in and I broke down. The impact of what happened suddenly hit me, and shaking her head Jane asked.
"Nora what is wrong with you now?"

I couldn't respond so Lanora answered.
"Aunt Jane I think my dad called and threatened my Mom."
She began to cry then Luther took over.

"Aunt Jane this is what happened, after my Mom got off the phone she ran into our rooms shouting that we had to leave the house right away, and when Julius began to ask her why--"

He too began to cry. Then Julius stepped in.

"This is how it went Aunt Jane."

"Mom didn't want to explain to us why we had to leave, so when I acted like I wasn't going to move as fast as she wanted me to, she shouted. 'If we don't hurry and get out of here, your father will be home in no time.' I knew she was serious. I know the last thing she would want is for something to happen to any of us."

He broke down and started to cry.

"I'm sorry Mom."

A few hours went by and Larry called with his usual sickening apologies. "Trust me Nora it's safe to come home. I swear to God that I'd never lay hands on you."

"Larry, as for the house being safe, I don't know how long it will be before you revert to your violent state. So, I'd rather play it safe for tonight."

While everyone else slept, I lay awake, unable to rest. It felt so good being out of the house, free of all the tension, and not wondering if I would live to see the break of another day.

CHAPTER TWENTY-NINE

I couldn't stay with Jane forever and returned home the next day. Larry was back to his games and one evening when I returned home I faced my biggest fear.

"I suggest that we put closure to the relationship between you and the children. The kids and I had a good talk last night and I'm still amazed at the outcome. Luckily, it worked in my favor. They've all requested to stay with me and not be associated with you at all. So now that you've got your freedom, why don't you just go back to your brother's house?"

I felt betrayed. My world was crumbling as Larry had succeeded in turning the kids against me. But knowing Larry it could be another smoke screen. I just could not accept what I was hearing.
So I retorted, "I don't believe a word you're saying. My children love me and I'm positive they didn't make such a request."

Turning to the kids he said, "Your mother cannot accept the fact that you kids have made a choice as to who you want to live with. So since she's not taking my word for it, why don't you all go ahead and give her the news one by one.
Julius came forward first:
"I want to live with Daddy."

I knew it was a lie. This child had endured some cruel beatings and severe mental abuse from Larry and had a hard time forgiving him. His mouth spoke the message yet his heart was saying something else.

Luther was next:
"Mommy, He made a long pause before continuing.
"I want to live with Daddy."

I could sense that he was trying to tell me something. As young as he was Luther was the only child to read the bible and pray everyday. I knew he was praying for God to reveal the truth to me.

It was Lanora's turn:
"With Daddy Mommy."
She said this in a great hurry and took one look at me and broke into tears."But I still love you." She sobbed. I knew that second part was unrehearsed and I could sense Larry's discomfort.

He shouted in an effort to regain control.
"Darrel it's your turn:"If everyone is going to live with Daddy, I guess I have to go too. But I'm going to miss you Mommy. Why can't you come with us?"

His pleading words plucked at my heartstrings. Larry knew that there was a special bond between Darrel and I, which developed from the days we lived at the group home. I knew this was just another attempt to destroy this bond but I was confident it was unbroken.

Patrick:
"I'll live with Daddy."
Now this child was the spitting image of his father and was often told. He never took it as a compliment but Patrick was easily influenced. Despite his looks, he loved me dearly.

Tanya:
"I want to live with Daddy too."
Well she was definitely the easiest to program. She was only carrying out orders and following her siblings.

The minute they were finished with their performance, Larry dismissed them as though they were little actors and actresses. With that sickening smirk on his face he turned to me.

"I hope you can handle it woman, you asked for it and you heard it for yourself. So the next move is yours"
I felt nothing but utter and absolute disgust for this pig. I looked him directly in the eyes and screamed.

"You're a stinking liar and you're going to regret this day."
I walked out of the house, got in my car and as soon as I put the car in reverse he ran up to me.

"If you think you're bad Nora, try fighting me for these kids. I promise, I'll be your worst nightmare."

Once more I went to Kevin's house to find refuge but he was not there. I fumbled in my pocketbook until I found the key he'd given me. I opened the door and went in. The constant stress had resulted in a terrible migraine that was hard for me to shake. The throbs were unbearable so I made it to Kevin's little medicine cabinet to find something for the pain. As I swung the glass door open, I couldn't help but glance at my haggard reflection.

'God, I look awful. I'm wasting away and I must get out of this self destructive relationship.' I was awakened by someone trying to unlock the door, suddenly the pain returned. 'Dear God, it must be Larry. But how did he get a key to Kevin's house?'
As I tried to solve the mystery, Kevin walked in.

"Nora are you okay?"
"I'm doing a lot better now that you're here. I was scared out of my wits thinking it was Larry."

"Nora, it's about time you stop being so afraid of this man. He's nothing but a bluff. God forgive me, but I hate him with a passion."

"Kevin I couldn't wait to talk to you, so what do you think happened with the kids?" I asked.

"I don't believe those children have turned against you Nora. They have better sense than that. You have a special relationship with each one of them and Larry would do anything in his power to break it. But the bond you have with those kids cannot be broken. Don't worry Larry's running out of games."

Poor Kevin was so exhausted during our conversation he just went out like a light. When I heard him snoring I decided I was going to leave quietly and return home.

The cool night breeze was like tonic to my aching body, as I drove home I experienced an inner strength and peace. When I approached the house and noticed that Larry's car was not there, I was relieved.

"Thank God he's gone."
I was uncertain what type of reception I'd get from the kids, but I imagined that they would all be asleep.

Before I could even get in the door the two eldest boys were waiting for me with open arms. Without a word said the mystery was solved. Luther informed me that they prayed and asked God to bring me back home. Julius said they were going to stay up until I returned, even if it meant staying up all night.

The night you slept at Uncle Kevin's, Daddy told us that you were planning to abandon us, because you no longer wanted to deal with the responsibility. He told each of us what to say when you came home and we had to rehearse it over and over until we got it right. He reminded us to stick to the plan."

"This was exactly what Uncle Kevin said. He told me you guys were only carrying out orders."

Over the next few weeks my brothers and sisters were ready to assist in moving the kids and myself in our own home. Of course the condition was that Larry could not move with us. That was perfect, as Larry had no choice now than to leave.

While Larry and I spoke the phone rang and as I answered I discovered that it was not my call, but it was Pamela Jakes, Larry's new love. I handed him the phone.

He took the receiver, "Oh no need to be sorry Pam, I can talk to you freely now. I've discussed the situation with Nora and she's very happy for us. Just to prove my point, why don't you go ahead and say hello to her. She'll be happy to speak with you."

Before I even had a chance to tell Larry that I didn't want to be a part of his love triangle he handed me the phone. For a second the line was dead then she timidly said.

"Hi."

I decided I'd be decent and give her my heartiest congratulations.
"Hi Pamela, this is Nora, Larry has said some nice things about you and I wish you both all the best. You're more than welcomed to have him and I hope you will be happy together."

I sensed her surprise at my response. "I hope things will work out for you and I'm sorry if I caused any problem but I really love Larry and I'll do everything to make him happy."

"Don't worry about me." I said.

CHAPTER THIRTY

The Realtor found the ideal town house and arranged to pick me up to see if it met my standards. When she arrived Larry insisted that he wanted to come along, so I would not be embarrassed I agreed for him to come. I loved it but it seemed like Larry loved it more. He took over the tour and even took the contract from the realtor and signed his name to it. I observed all this but when I handed her the down payment I requested that the receipt was written in my name only.

When we returned home Larry informed me that he was going to be moving with us. He went on to remind me that it was his name on the lease agreement. Larry had not realized that his tired tricks had gotten old and this time I was one step ahead. Later that day I met with the realtor to sign a new agreement and set a date to move in the house.

I now needed twenty-four hundred dollars in order to move. It was frightening especially seeing that I was not working. I called my brother in Canada who promised to assist in whatever way he could. He told me all he had was credit cards but he was going to send me to someone in Miami who could help me. I asked Kevin to accompany me to meet Lenworth's friend, a Jamaican millionaire who lived on Miami Beach.

Lenworth briefed the man about my distressed situation and my abuse. As soon as I entered his house the man spoke in the Jamaican dialect.

"Your brother is a good fren a'mine an tell me your 'usban is a mad man who abuse you an de children dem. Listen lady, I don't stan' for dat blood-clate. A man like dat deserve to die. I would love to mek an example out of him. Jus give me de okay an I'll take care of everything."
"What do you mean?" I nervously asked.

"Well we can start by breakin' a few bones or if yuh prefer for me to jus kill him I won't av' a problem wid dat eider. Yuh understan' where a comin' from?"

"Not really, because I didn't come here for that," I answered.

"I didn't tink so, because you don't hav de guts to do it anyway. But if yuh hav a change of heart jus pik up de phone an call, yuh don't even hav to com back down here."

Kevin looked at me then glanced at his watch. I got the message. We both stood up together.

"Ok sir, sorry to waste your time, but I have a conscience and I have to sleep at night."

"Yeh, I hope yuh liv to sleep at nite."

When Kevin and I drove off, he commented.

"Do you realize if you were not a God fearing person you could have easily gotten rid of Larry today. Dis man look like he's head of de 'Jamaican Mafia' and I can't believe Lenworth sent you to him. Killing was the only thing on his mind. Nora I know Larry's a mad man, but the last thing I want is his blood on your hands. Let God deal with him in His time"

After I dropped Kevin off at work, I was so drained that I stopped by his apartment to get a little rest. The moment I laid down, Larry called.

"So tell me Nora, did you get the whole amount from your brother's millionaire friend?"

'If only Larry knew.' I thought.
So I chuckled then answered.
"Larry you should be thankful today that I know God. Because if not, I cold easily have had you hurt. But I refuse to go that route."

Before I was finished Larry was cursing everyone in my family. I was tired so I abruptly hung up the phone. Within ten minutes there was a loud knock on the door, although his office was approximately twenty minutes away. I knew it was Larry so when I opened the door he stormed in.
"So you an your damn brothers are planning to get rid of me? Let me tell you, I'll kill every last one of them, then turn myself in. You hear me bitch. Here I

am thinking I'm safe with you while you're plotting to kill me. You're a wicked, wicked bitch."

He grabbed me by the shoulders and pushed me against the wall. He caught my upper arm and squeezed it as if he was trying to break every bone. I was in severe pain.

I fought to get away from his grip, but he was too strong. I was pinned down by his hold. A surge of blood rushed to my head and I slammed my high heels into his shin. Immediately he let me go as he held up his injured foot.
.
"What the hell have you done? You must be out of your fucking mind. If you try that with me again I swear I'll kill you with my bare hands. I don't think you realize who you're fucking with."

He lunged at me and pinned my back against the wall. I fought to break away. But when I glanced in his eyes and saw that killer look I knew I was in trouble and was no match for him. My one defense had never failed me so I screamed on top of my voice.

"Help! Somebody help me!"

In the midst of the struggle, I heard sirens coming towards the apartment. He quickly released me and started straightening up the living room. So attempting to sound composed he said.

"I know you love your brother an' all, but if you ever mention that I even as much as touch you, I'll have the immigration on his ass and before you know it, he'll be deported. Immigration is nasty business. Do you understand?"

With absolute hatred for this pig I humbly answered.
"Yes."

When the cops entered the room Larry was calm and relaxed and informed them that we were only having a domestic dispute. He assured them that everything was under control.

The minute the cops left Larry returned to his mean ugly ways.

"Oh you thought you had me there for a moment, didn't you? Let me show you what I think of you bitch."
With that he spat in my face and walked out the door. I shook my head in shame.

I knew that was the last straw. My arms were bruised also and I couldn't tolerate physical abuse.

Later that night he called. I was in no mood for another set of apologies and was about to hang up the phone.

"I have nothing to say to you Larry. Just leave me al---"
"No, no Nora, please don't hang up. I want only a minute. Please. I don't know if you're aware of this, but shortly after we'd left the attorney's office the other day, I called to stop the divorce proceedings again. However, these instructions did not get to Al. And after today's unfortunate incident I came home to find the divorce papers in the mailbox. Al signed the papers so I guess you and I need to sign so we can once and for all put this to an end. I know you always said the day I lay hands on you is the day our marriage will be over. I guess you're right, it's now up to you to accept or contest this divorce."

"I have no interest in contesting this divorce my only interest is to get you out of my life."

The divorce wouldn't be final until the following year so until that time we would be separated. I couldn't wait for the new-year to come and to be finally rid of this incredible burden.

There was stillness on the other line and I hung up the phone. I sat in the living room and reflected. I felt saddened when I pondered on the wasted years with Larry. However, I felt victorious in knowing that the chains were finally broken and there was nothing that could get in the way of my freedom.

CHAPTER THIRTY-ONE

Finally, Larry and I were to go our separate ways. I decided to take the mature approach and resolve the matter concerning custody of the children. While I waited for him to come home I gathered all his personal belongings and packed them in garbage bags. When he arrived home he thought it was garbage and was at the verge of throwing them out. I was dripping with sarcasm.

"I suggest you don't do that, because you'd be left without a shirt on your back if you did."

He was not amused. I tried to talk to him about his role in supporting the children but he said I should allow him to get situated first then he'd take care of his responsibilities. I didn't believe.

As he prepared to leave he came into the kitchen looking dejected.
"I know this may be asking a lot especially as I'd refused to sign the HRS forms stipulating that I was an absentee parent. Well the truth is your cupboards are filled with food and I have no money to buy food and neither does Pamela. Yeah! I know you can't believe, but it's true. Pamela is a struggling physician who left her big practice back home and cannot do anything here without a license. So can you please help me out with some groceries?"

My mouth fell to the ground and it was a while before I could speak.
"Larry I cannot believe what I'm hearing, but I'm not a spiteful person. As long as I'm not depriving my kids, I'll be woman enough to give you some groceries. I opened my cupboard and gave him what I could.

Then he went to my phone and called his Pamela.
"Hi Pamela, I'm all set and ready to go. How long will it take you to get here?" No

problem, I'll be waiting for you."

Within a half an hour she was at the front door. Larry displayed some bold behavior. "Honey, that was quick, why don't you come in and have a seat while I load up the car?"

Larry's head had gotten too big for his body, and I couldn't figure out what he was trying to prove by having her come in to sit in my living room, in my sofa. Her presence in the house immediately changed Larry's temperament. He became arrogant and self-centered.

I thought to myself here I am allowing this man to bring this adulteress into my home. So I addressed Larry.

"On second thought I'd prefer for her to wait outside."
I couldn't believe that I said it. Pamela apologized.

"It was wrong for me to come in." She stood to her feet. Larry grabbed her hand and they headed towards the door. Suddenly he stopped, turned around and looked back at me with the six children standing by my side.

"Let me tell you something Nora, you and your six kids can get the fuck out of my life. They won't amount to anything. They'll all drop out of school and end up on drugs. None of you will EVER amount to anything. Come on Pamela; let's get the hell out of here."

The door slammed shut, it was the final crescendo in a disjointed symphony. There was total silence in the house. So this was it? No tears were shed, not even tears of joy—so simple, so final. Those words culminated fourteen years of pain, anguish, frustration and deception. Should I have felt elated? No. I was saddened, not at Larry being gone, but for all the wasted years and the six innocent lives, for which I had to fend.

As I sat there I pulled myself together, determined to fight my way out of this plight. Together the children and I knelt in prayer asking God to direct our lives from that day on and to give us strength and wisdom to prepare for the challenges ahead. Our most fervent prayer was for me to find a job. When we were through we hugged each other realizing that for the first time as a family, peace and true love had finally entered our lives.

When Larry left, fear left with him and immediately a weight was lifted from my shoulders. Finally, we were free from living a life of fear. I was on my own and had to provide for these children because after that spectacle I knew Larry wouldn't.

Everyone camped in my room that night. Look what I'd been missing all these years, precious moments with my children. As I got up early the next morning to use the bathroom, Julius jumped up…
"Are you alright Mom?"

I was still feeling some pain from Larry's attack. But after a peaceful night's rest I wasn't focusing on it. However, Julius's question brought the pain back to full consciousness.

"Yes J. I'm alright except for my shoulders, they hurt so bad."

"Can I take a look at it?" He asked.
"Sure."

I saw the astonishment on his face as he examined my shoulders.
"Mommy, what's wrong with your shoulders, the whole thing is black and blue. Did Daddy do this?"

"Honey, you'll never live to see your mother black and blue again. This will be the first and last time."

His voice betrayed his pain.
"Mommy, if Daddy ever comes back here and touches you, I swear I'll kill him."

I knew from the sound of his voice that he meant what he said.
"Julius, one of these days, ask God to help you forgive your dad. It's not good for us to harbor hate in our hearts."

"I don't know about that Mom. Remember his famous quote, children are to be seen and not heard. Well those days ended yesterday," he coldly replied.

I hoped that my abusive marriage would not have any adverse effects on my children. I was going to teach them love by loving them. I wanted to be their best friend and their hero. I was going to spend time and pray with them, play with them, do chores and home work with them. I wished I could just commit myself to them and make a full time job out of raising them, but that was not realistic.

I had to go out and find a real job as it required money for us to move into the townhouse and to raise my children. I made a list of my brothers, sisters and close relatives who had promised to help if I left Larry. I was going to put them to the test but I was going to secure a job before soliciting help.

Within seven days I had to find a job, raise $2,400 and move into our new home. Challenging, but I knew it could be done. The kids prayed asking God to provide a job for me and when they had finished praying Luther reassured me that God was going to answer their prayers.

Later that day I called my ex boss at the fitness center to inquire about vacancies. She was thrilled to receive my call and informed me that there was a managerial position open and she would like to make me an offer. I was beside myself as this was too good to be true. I was really interested to go and fill out the necessary paper work since I had so little time working with. In conversation, I inquired about two managers whom I had a good relationship with prior to leaving the company. I was told they'd both left and was working for Nutri-Health. She sensed my concern and told me she was confident that this was the right time to join the company, as sales were at a record high. I thanked her for her time and told her I'd have an answer by tomorrow. Right before she got off the phone she discussed my salary and offered me a little more than what I was earning when I left. However, I needed to make more money as now I was a full fledged single mom. So I eagerly contacted the girls at Nutri-Health to see if anything was available and more importantly to discuss compensation.

The minute I hung up, I called operator assistance for the phone number, when I made the call I immediately recognized Tara's voice.

"Hi Nora, what have you and Larry been up to these days? I haven't heard from you guys in over a year, and how are all those kids of yours doing anyway?"

"Tara, the kids are doing fine. But as for Larry and I, we're no longer together and"

Without even having a chance to finish she interrupted.

"How can you manage with all those kids by yourself? My goodness, what are you going to do?"

"Well, the first thing I need is a job, one that will pay me well and provide good health benefits. Do you have anything open right now?"

"You might be in luck Nora, because a few days ago I heard that there was an opening for a senior sales rep, that's like an entry level position for management."
"Do you have any idea how much it's paying?"

"I really don't, but I can call my boss and call you back in a few. Let me have your number."

We hung up the phone and within a few minutes she called back. She scheduled an interview with her boss at 9:00 AM the following morning. I was confident that I was going to land one of the two jobs so I got on the phone and called my siblings. Before the end of the night I had commitments for $2,400 that would be wired to me within twenty-four hours. I told my family that I'd secured a job and would start working right after we moved.

I took sometime to prepare myself for the interview and though I'd not been out on the job market for a while I felt very confident. My children encouraged me and cheered me on all night, telling me that since I was no longer under their father's control they knew I could do it.

Julius said, "Mommy all you need is one break and you'll move right to the top. Don't worry about the kids, Luther and I will help out so you won't ever have to miss work."

Julius was beginning to assume the father's role.

"You guys are great. I promise I won't let you down. With God's help I will get one of these jobs."

The following morning I arrived fifteen minutes before the interview. I believed that I looked and sounded professional. When I left the area supervisor's office she shook my hand and told me to expect a call in three days. An hour after returning home she called and offered me the job. I was ecstatic. Things were moving fast and everything was working in my favor.

Later on that day I made several trips to the check-cashing store to pick up monies coming in from my relatives. Before the end of that day I collected a total of $2,400. We gave God thanks as He had answered all our prayers.
We spent the rest of the week and packed our belongings and I also got my clothes ready for work.

As I lay in my bed that night, Luther walked in the room.
"Mommy, are you sleeping?"
"No honey, what's up?" I asked.
"Mommy do you realize that God has answered every single one of our prayers? Maybe, not in our time, but He did. Mommy you're going to do so well at your new job. But remember, it's going to be in God's time."

"Luther, you have no idea how much you kids mean to me. That's why I have to succeed, because of you guys. And by the way Luther thanks for your prayers over the years. You never stopped praying I really believe that you've got a direct line to God. Thank you for the encouraging words honey, I love you. Goodnight."

For me everything was going well. I had a new job, new house and newly found freedom. I was filled with excitement and anticipation towards a bright future and I could only conceptualize success. For the first time in my life I was faced with a decision as to what I wanted to do with my life. Well, one of my top priorities was my commitment to my children in helping them to recover from the mental and physical abuse, and love them unconditionally. My goal was to take these broken kids and with the help of God reshape their lives and help them become strong, confident and resilient. But most importantly I was going to teach them to love.

CHAPTER THIRTY-TWO

It had been six months since Larry left and I had not received a dime towards child support. However, one thing I could count on was Larry's telephone calls. It was 2:30 in the morning when the phone rang.

"Hello"

"Nora I'd like to borrow the car tomorrow. I've found a job in New York and I'll be leaving in a week. I need to move my things out of Pamela's house."

I didn't like the request but I really needed some financial assistance and I hoped that the plans to move to New York would work. So I agreed.

Larry picked up the car the following morning. He was excited about relocating to New York. My day at work progressed as usual then I received a call from Larry about five o'clock.

"Nora, it's me. It's such a great feeling to be in my own bed again."
I had a quick relapse.
"What are you talking about?" I asked.

"Nora, relax, I'm calling you from our bedroom, at the townhouse. This is what I've been missing. Home. Home sweet home!"

"You jerk! You piece of crap! Get out of my house or I'll have the cops over there, if you're not out in three minutes. Moreover, you'll miss your flight because it's a little after five."

"I wasn't going to New York I was hoping that you'd give me a chance, but I see you've become hard and cold and you have no mercy for me."

Even though he was no longer with me he was still playing with my emotions and I was very upset at myself. This should not have happened.

"You're going to regret this day" he said'"because you have no idea what you want. This might be your last chance for us to reunite as a family."

"I'm very confident about what I don't want and I DON'T WANT YOU! Get out of my house before the cops come and throw you out, go get a job you broke bastard."

"You piece of shit."With that he slammed the receiver in my ear.

Larry did not return the car that night and I had no way of contacting him. The following morning I had to get a ride to work, during the course of the day I borrowed a coworker's car, to run home and fix lunch for the children. Shortly after I arrived I received a call from my office informing me that Larry had just left the center and they believe he was on his way to my house. The minute I hung up the phone he was at my door. In his arrogant tone he came by to let me know that he was taking the car.

"Look how unfair you are. You're not supporting the kids and I'm not even pressuring you, because as long as I can work I'll not beg you for a dime. But in order for me to do this I must have the car."

He laughed scornfully.
"So you're finally coming to the realization that you do need me? Sorry to burst your bubble Nora, but you can't make it without me. You've been riding so high, now I'll watch you fall flat on your face."

I was in a state of panic."How can you take something that belongs to me? I need the car for work and I have no other way of getting Tanya to and from the sitter."

"First this car never belonged to you. It wasn't a mistake why your name was never put on the title. So don't cry your little eyes out, all I'm doing is claiming what is rightfully mine. And as for Tanya, you can throw her in a garbage can, for all I care."

That did it. He had gone too far. I wouldn't have him talking bad about my children. It was just them and I struggling. All Larry did since he left was cause more pain. But I had to put an end to that and sever all ties with him.

I barked at him. "Get out. Get out you stinking dog. Take your car and get out of my life." I grabbed the duplicate key from off the key holder and threw it at him.

"Here take it you jerk."

Childishly he dangled his key in my face.
"I'm sure your family will get you out of this bind too."

"Get out, you're a two time loser. You'll never be a real man."

For eight long weeks I had no transportation and was never late or absent from work. I was able to save $300 to buy a 1981 Buick Century from my brother's neighbor. There were some good things about this deal, Larry couldn't borrow or take this car from me, but better yet, there were no monthly payments.

CHAPTER THIRTY-THREE

It was the beginning of a new school year and Larry did not contribute a pencil to the kids' school supplies. His family was disappointed in his lack of support, so they assisted in buying clothes for the kids to return to school. Now all six kids were in school and things were a lot more manageable.

Julius landed his first job at E & M carwash. The owner Eugene was affectionately called G, a comical, caring man who'd have liked to provide jobs for all the boys in the neighborhood. This he knew was impossible but he gave young boys an opportunity to work at an early age, teaching them how to become independent.

G, understood the struggles I faced as a single mom and assured me that as long as my boys were reliable and willing to work, they'd be guaranteed a job at the car wash. I was grateful that Julius could work and make some extra money.
I didn't take his money, but it's one less person for me to buy shoes and clothes for and it taught Julius from a very early age the importance of establishing proper work ethics.

"Listen Nora, whatever I can do to help you I will. By the way Julius was telling me about his little brother Luther, he says he's a hard worker, do you think he's too young to come out?"

"G, he just turned twelve, but acts like he's twenty four."

"How's his grades?" he asked.
"Straight A student." I answered.

"I think I like him already. Bring him with Julius next week, but pick him up half day so I can break him in slowly."

"Thanks G, that's two less to buy clothes and shoes for. By the time Darrel and Patrick get hired I can start putting some money in the bank,"I said.

"Nothing's wrong with that Nora. But let me ask you a personal question, how you let your husban' get away with this type of stuff. This man needs to support his kids or you throw his ass in jail. It's as simple as that. A lot of people serve time for less serious stuff. Nora believe me that's messed up, you need to make an example of this man an' don't let him get away with it. I just hate a man who don't take care of his kids."

"G, I really don't have the time to go to legal aid and wait all day to see an attorney. I cannot miss a day at work because every dime of my money is accounted for. The truth is, I really can't afford to hire an attorney to represent me."

"Do me a favor an' find an attorney, then we can talk."

"Okay G, after the holidays I'll start looking."

"Speaking of holidays I hear Christmas is on Julius this year. I will let him work from open till close everyday during the holidays and on weekends, so he can make enough money to buy gifts for his brothers and sisters. Tell me, how many other kids his age would do something like that? I tell you, you're doing a good job as a single mom Nora, this boy would give his life for you."

"No, I would give my life for them G. These kids are all I've got. I could stay here and talk with you all day, but I have to go deliver my fruit cakes to some of the local restaurants around town. That's how I get to make a little extra money during the holidays."

"Check this out Nora, you save the money from the sale of the fruit cakes and after the holidays whatever you've saved I'll match it. That way you can get your divorce for the new year."

It sounded like a plan. So I looked at him and said,"Deal?"

He looked back at me and answered,"Deal."

Every dime that Julius earned was used to purchase gifts for his siblings. This was something he'd always dreamt of doing.
"Mommy, I've always wanted to know what it felt like to have a Christmas tree.

All these years and we've never celebrated the holidays."

The following week we started our shopping spree. Julius was filled with pride when he took out his hard earned money to pay for the gifts. We'd hurry home dash into my bedroom, lock the door and wrap the gifts. When he placed them under the tree, everyone was amazed. There was so much happiness and laughter among the kids. Because of Julius our family was experiencing the true spirit of Christmas for the first time.

One night after all the kids were gone to bed, I sat by the Christmas tree with tears in my eyes amazed at what a fifteen year old could accomplish. Yet when his father left at thirty-eight years old he could not even afford to leave with his own food. I just sat and thought about life and its ironies, when I felt a gentle hand on my shoulder. Julius came and sat next to me.

"Mom do you feel anything?" he asked. "All my years as a child this is all I've ever wanted. Even if I never do this again, I just want to experience it at least once in my life."

I used some money from the cake sales and bought a gift for each of the kids. But for Julius, I sacrificed and rewarded him for his kind deeds. The kids were thrilled on Christmas Eve. In all, there were close to thirty gifts under the tree. During the entire night the music of Nat King Cole complimented the festivity. The only lights in the living room were those from the tree.

When the alarm went off the next morning I jumped up only to find all the kids already piled in the bathrooms hurriedly brushing their teeth. We all gathered around the tree and prayed, thanking God for using Julius to bring happiness to our family.

Before long everyone was opening their gifts and earnestly thanking Julius. Within minutes, the entire living room was covered with wrapping paper, ribbons and toys. All the kids were laughing and playing and the true spirit of Christmas was shared. My thoughts strayed for a while when I saw how much my kids had missed over the years because of Larry's manipulation and selfishness.

CHAPTER THIRTY-FOUR

Months after the new-year I realize that Julius wasn't the same. His spirit was not as up beat as usual. It seemed like he had a lot on his mind. It was his turn to share.

"Julius what's up?"
"Mom things aren't looking good for me right now. With my current GPA I doubt if I'll be able to graduate high school. Therefore, I'm just letting you know that college is definitely out of the question."

I didn't want Julius to jeopardize his education because he felt responsible to help raise his brothers and sisters. I knew this was going to be a tough discussion so I had to choose my words carefully.

"Julius you've just completed the 10th grade and you still have two more years before you graduate. Right now my focus is for you to graduate high school. To every problem there is a solution, so we need to find a way to get you back on track."

He wasn't convinced.

"Mom, let's be realistic. If I couldn't get my grades up in two years what makes you think I'll be able to do it now?"
"First of all with the help of God and a desire to succeed you can do anything. Here's the plan. I'll be at your school tomorrow to enroll you in summer school."

Before I had a chance to finish he interrupted.
"How am I suppose to go to summer school when I have to work at the car wash?"

"Hold that thought Julius. Let me clarify something right here and now. Before you started working at the car wash, I was able to manage and I provided the things you needed, right? In our family working part time is a privilege. It's an opportunity for you to become self-reliant and to be in a position to purchase the things you need. It's as simple as that. If you were serious about working in the summer, you'd have gotten better grades. So the bottom line is, since you do not have passing grades you will not be able to work at the car wash and you will have to attend summer school instead."

He did not respond and I was not certain if I was reaching him.
"Let me ask you a question Julius, how important is college to you?"

"It's important," he replied.

"What level of commitment are you prepared to make to get into college?"

He didn't answer, but with his face cupped in his hands, I saw the tears seeping thru his fingers.

"Honey, you have to believe that this is a workable plan."

I hugged him but quickly dried the tears from my eyes, as I had to remain strong.

"Julius, I promise that once you stick to this plan you will start 11th grade in the fall and you won't be left behind. Time is of the essence and remember every second counts. Keeping in mind that this objective is two fold; being promoted to 11th grade and getting into college."

I kissed his forehead and as I turned around to leave, he hugged me.

"I love you Mom…I won't let you down."

"I love you too."

Three times a week we gathered as a family to talk about issues affecting our lives. It was important to me to provide an environment for the children to vent and have their views heard. I felt that this exercise helped the kids to learn to express themselves and not be afraid to speak up. Sometimes I would lead the session by talking to the kids about life and its challenges. I would talk to them about developing a winning attitude and the ability to overcome difficulties.

One day I was drawn to an article in USA today entitled, 'Black women see dreams die.' After reading the article I couldn't wait to get home to share what I had read with my children.

Ironically the single mom who was mentioned also had six children. The photograph had five of the six, as the second child, eighteen was in jail. I started out by reading some excerpts from the story.

"Last year 51% of black children had no fathers in their homes, a record high rate that has cultural and economic ramifications that could last for generations. Children in single parent families are economically disadvantaged and that hurts their opportunities. It makes it harder for black children to achieve economic mobility."

For this single mother that I was reading about, single motherhood meant watching her three children drop out of high school, one by one, and feeling that only a father could have persuaded them to stay. The oldest son said, "just didn't believe school would make a difference, looking around at better dressed white class mates, I just felt I was black and no matter what, I would fail."

After fruitless struggles to control her oldest son, his mother kicked him out of the house. He stayed with friends in hotels and on the street. He returned home still looking for work, often being rejected.

"It seemed like my life was going nowhere." He said. But he is now at a pivotal position. His girlfriend is pregnant, potentially another black, single mother.'

I passed the article around, so the kids could take a look. Julius looked at the picture as he commented, "The oldest son, dropped out of school, couldn't find a job and on top of that got his girlfriend pregnant. Listen guys, that's not going to be us. That's not our story! I've been doing really well in summer school and it looks like I'm going to pass the eleventh grade. After all Mom has done I'm not going to let her down. I'm definitely not failing, I wouldn't even know how to fail. There's no justification for failure, especially for black people. But someone should have told this to sperm donor."

My eyes opened wide.

"What did you say Julius?"

They were all laughing. But I needed some clarification. Luther looked on Julius, as if to say.

'You got busted.'
Julius was bold as he defined the meaning.

"Mom, Larry is a sperm donor. His goal was to have lots of kids and not support any of them. And that goes for any man who can walk away from his family without thinking about their well being. In our opinion Mom, that's who a sperm donor is."

All the kids cheered Julius with the exception of Luther. Even little Tanya was laughing as if she understood.
"Guys, it sounds harsh, but you do have a point."

Luther showed more interest in the statistical portion of the article.
"Mom I'm really interested in this quote. 'Children in single parent families are economically disadvantaged, and this part about, 'It makes it harder for black children to achieve economic mobility.

"While that might be true, this will not happen with this family. It doesn't have to happen to every family. In our family we struggle then we overcome, and that cycle goes on for a period, but one day the struggles will subside and the victories will be greater. I'm confident that in the near future we will be economically strong and we won't have all these financial problems. The key is to stay focused and don't give up."

CHAPTER THIRTY-FIVE

Despite my determination my divorce proceedings had stalled. It was approaching three months since my attorney first made attempts to contact Larry, but without luck.

'Three months of precious time wasted, that's enough I have to take matters in my own hands, even if I have to serve the papers myself.'

My thoughts were going wild and time was running out.

Larry's intent was to frustrate my attorney, so they would become fed up and drop the case. Up to this point they had made several attempts to serve the summons but Larry was like a fugitive, they couldn't pin him down.

I reflected on the article I shard with the kids and since they were not going to receive any financial support from Larry I wanted to make a clean break and continue the challenges of single parenting on my own. I didn't want to have any excuse for failure. So I realized that one of the surest ways to succeed as a single parent was to commit to my children my determination to win and by doing so, they won't allow me to fail.

So it was my time to be tested and with the help of God I knew I was going to succeed. Like everything else in my life I formulated a plan, I outlined the steps and I put it in action.

I told everyone who knew Larry, that if they saw him they should let him know that it's extremely important for him to contact me. Finally he got one of the messages. Within twenty-four hours, I received a call from him, asking what it was that I needed. I tried my best to suppress my anger as this man was playing hide and seek with my children's lives. Though challenging, I managed to remain calm.

"Hi Larry, where've you been? I was wondering if you had left town."

He responded with some anxiety in his voice.
"Nora, I wonder if I'm hearing right. Am I detecting some sort of care and concern in your voice? So I guess absence does make the heart grow fonder. Tell me Nora, are you having a change of heart?"

"Larry, let's just say, I'm concerned. Can we meet tomorrow at my job so we can talk about this? I must see you."

"Sure, I'll meet you tomorrow evening. But I can't figure out what could be so important."

Later on that day he called to advise me that after reviewing his schedule he realized that he could not fit me in.

'Gosh, what am I going to do now?' I wondered.

"Larry I really wish you'd stop playing with my head. All I'm trying to do is get on with this divorce. Because God forbid, if something were to happen to me right now, you'd be the prime suspect."

"What the hell are you talking about Nora, is someone threatening you or something. And why am I just hearing about this?"

"Larry, how are you supposed to know when I've made numerous attempts to reach you? The police have been after me for your number."

"What the fuck is going on?"

"Larry, I'm not at liberty to disclose any information at this time as I really don't know where I stand with you."

He sounded concerned, "Do me a favor and arrange for the sheriff to meet me at your office tomorrow evening at 5:00 P.M. so we can get this over with once and for all. Because I'd be dammed before I get framed for something I didn't do."

I received a call from Larry at 3:45 PM the day we were scheduled to meet. He said he was unable to keep the appointment as he couldn't get a ride. I was prepared for this so I replied, "That's no problem Larry, just tell me where you are and I'll come and get you."

There was a long pause and he stuttered as he replied.
"Well...It's raining cats and dogs up here and I--I—wou--wouldn't want you to come all the way up here, in this rain. We're better off just setting another appointment."

"There'll be no other appointments Larry the sheriff will be meeting us as planned. So we don't have a minute to waste. It's not my first time driving in rain and it won't be the last. What's the address?"

"You're so damned stubborn, never in my life have I seen a woman as determined as you. Alright, I'll make this real easy. Meet me at the Sheraton Hotel on Coral Ridge Drive."

The kids had overheard my conversation and they pleaded with me not to go.
"Mommy, that's stupid to go and meet Daddy. How can you trust him after all the things he's done?"
Lenora's pleads brought back some of the abuse to focus but my mind was already made up.

"Listen kids, all I'm going to ask you to do is pray that God will protect me and allow Larry to be successfully served his divorce papers." Luther was concerned but seemed like he admired my courage. "Mom, we'll be praying for you and remember God is on your side. Don't worry about us, we'll be fine."

As I rushed thru the doors I noticed that Julius was missing.
"Where's Julius, tell him to pray for me too."

As I reversed, Julius burst out with a funny laugh from behind me.
"Not only will I pray for you, but I'll be right there with you."

I could not believe this child was in the van.

"Did you think I was going to let you go by yourself? No way. I'll be there to protect you if you need me to."

I smiled at him, being touched by his gesture.
"You're special Julius and I love you."

We drove for a long time before seeing the hotel. I turned in the main driveway and pulled up in front, expecting to see Larry. My heart sank as there was no sign of him outside or in the lobby. I turned away to leave the lobby when I felt compelled to inquire about Larry at the front desk.

"Excuse me, but would you happen to have a Larry Bell staying here?"

Without even looking him up on the computer the clerk replied.
"We sure do. Would you like me to ring his room?"

Trying to hide my shock, I replied.
"Yes, thank you."

When he answered the phone I sensed his surprise.
"Larry, I'm down stairs. Was I not suppose to meet you at the front of the hotel?"

"Yes Nora, but I still can't believe you're here already. I'll be down in a minute."

The minute turned into ten and I was about to call the room again when I saw Larry coming out of the elevator. I could tell from his body language that he was going against his will.

"I know we're going to miss the sheriff. We had a 5:00 o'clock appointment, it's now 5:15 and we're 45 minutes away. This doesn't make sense. But you'll see for yourself that it's a waste of time."

When he opened the door of the van and saw Julius, he was furious.
"Why was it necessary for him to come---?"
Before I had a chance to answer he continued.
"I guess you need your body guard eh."

I didn't respond, so Julius replied.
"I just felt like coming for the ride, is there something wrong with that?"

His father remained silent. By this time my beeper was vibrating every five minutes, but I had no way of returning the calls. My only focus was to get to our destination safely and in record time, Larry asked Julius a few questions.

"So how are you guys doing in school?"

"What does it matter to you?" Julius asked defiantly.

Larry realized that this was no longer the little boy he once terrorized and ceased asking him questions. "Well Nora, I guess this is the end."

"Larry I cannot speak for you, but for me, this is the beginning. This divorce will be the final step in becoming free."

He tried his wild stare that use to intimidate me but this time it had no effect whatsoever. When I pulled into the parking lot at my office I was forty five minutes late. Thankfully the sheriff's car was parked outside. This was the moment we'd all been waiting for, after two years of prolonging the divorce, the day had finally come. The sheriff walked up to him and informed him that he was being served with a summons for divorce, child support and a restraining order. The latter was unexpected, and he retorted.

"Nora. You liar. You lied to me."

"I'll explain on the way back." I said.

We walked back to the van. Larry appeared very confused as he shuffled through the papers, not knowing which ones to read first. As he came across the restraining order he shouted.

"Nora you lied to me. How can you stop me from seeing my children?"

"It's easy Larry; you don't support these kids so why do you think you have the right to see them?"

He was fuming, but now that the papers were served there was nothing holding me back. I felt courageous with an unusual sense of freedom. Larry was still on the restraining order.

"I resent you having the law restrain me from seeing my children. It's not fair"

"Life isn't fair and I could spend the next twenty four hours and tell you about the different challenges I've had to face in providing for the children single handedly. But I won't. I'd rather save the energy to work, love and nurture them. I'm about results not about wasting time and making excuses."

"I can see that you've been brainwashed into this, 'Woman's lib shit,' but you can talk until you're blue in the face. It's the man who runs things, and I'll take that to my grave."

"Larry, believe what you will, it doesn't matter. Since you run things you should see to it that your children are taken care of. That's the manly thing to do. With your ego, you should never give another man the privilege of supporting them. You need to stand your ground and once and for all be a man about it."

"So I suppose if I don't, you'll throw me in jail, right?" He inquired.

"Are you implying that you don't plan to?" I asked. He didn't respond so I continued.

"I would not willfully put you in jail but I have no control over the law if you break it."

After much discussion, we arrived at the hotel. Larry ignored me but turned to Julius and said good-bye, I watched him stroll into the hotel, his shoulders stooped, looking completely lost.

As I drove off, Julius hopped in the front seat and grabbed my hand.
"Mom I'm so proud of you, I never knew I'd live to see the day that you'd stand up to Larry. I'm so glad I was here so I could hear all this for myself.

CHAPTER THIRTY-SIX

Two weeks went by then I received a call from Larry. He informed me that he was really moving to New York this time and requested to stop by to see the children. With the restraining order enforced I wanted to ensure that the children had an interest in seeing him before I agreed for him to come by.

As I hung up the phone, I realized their decision was already made because together they shouted, "The answer is no."

I was not going to coerce them or justify why their father should come by. So I waited for Larry's call.

When I received the call he was in high spirits, "So Nora, what time can I stop by."

"Larry I suggest you call the children when you get to New York."

"Come on Nora it's not time for games, I see you're in the mood to play, but I'll be there shortly. It shouldn't take me more than thirty minutes or so."

"I'm not trying to be funny. But the kids are not interested in seeing you right now."

"What!" He exclaimed. "Put Julius on the phone."

This child was no longer afraid to express himself and informed his dad of their decision. He said his father ended the conversation sounding bitter. He thought that I was the one who had influenced their choice.

Despite Larry's resentment towards me I was adamant that my sons were taught the importance of respecting others, especially women. I would have loved for my boys to have their father as their role model. But I realized a role model was measured in the quality of one's life, their character, values, morals and achievements. Gender was not a criteria.

The following day I received a call from my attorney to inform me that a date was set for the hearing. I immediately made some calls to Larry's family in New York to try to locate him. I was unsuccessful, but a few days later Larry called.

I shared the information with him and asked if he was planning on being in court. "I'm not sure if I'm going to be there but what is more surprising to me is that you're still going through with this divorce. You and I know that this is not what God wants, so why don't you just drop it?"

I ignored him, as he had no idea what this meant to me.

The day finally came. I woke up feeling very positive knowing that by the end of the day, I'd be totally emancipated. Free from mental slavery and finally free from the link that connected me to Larry. Free to be who I wanted to be and what I wanted to become. Free to love my children unconditionally. Free-Free-Free.

Jane accompanied me to the courthouse. She sensed my anxiety and implored me to be calm. We arrived fifteen minutes early.

Within minutes my case was called. I looked around and there was no sign of Larry. In a matter of seconds my fate would be decided. The judge wore her spectacles at the tip of her nose, reminding me of an old high school teacher.

As she called the court to order, I closed my eyes in silent prayer. Then I was standing before her with my attorney. He presented the case and she spent a few minutes reviewing the documents. Finally she spoke.

"Are you Nora Faith Bell?"

"Yes I am your Honor."

"Are you definite in your petition to end the union with Larry Bell, your lawful spouse?"

"Yes I am your Honor."
"Are you satisfied that the union with Larry Bell is totally and irreconcilably broken?"
"Yes I am your Honor."

"Thank you. You may be seated."

As I sat down I felt somewhat nervous. I wondered if I had said something wrong. I thought the judge would have asked me more questions, as the process seemed very brief. My attorney moved closer to her and their conversation was to the point. They exchanged smiles and she requested that I stand again. This time she straightened her glasses, cleared her throat and smiled warmly at me.
Then I heard the words that will be forever etched in my mind.
"Nora Faith Bell, based on your petition and this court's review thereof, this court on my authority, declares your union with Larry Bell dissolved. This is a result of his desertion of you and his children and also as a result of irreconcilable differences."

I was in a daze. I heard the words being repeated over and over again---"Union with Larry Bell dissolved—dissolved—dissolved--."
For a minute my mind strayed and I quickly recapped the fourteen years.

'Am I finally free? Can I do what I want with my life?'
I was jolted back to my senses by the judge's words.
"Mrs. Bell, are you still here with us?"

"I'm sorry your Honor, I was ju--."

"I understand. There's no need to explain. I was saying in response to your petition, this court has agreed to:

-Payment of respondent of $1,100.00 per month child support. All payments must be made through the courts until the last child attains the age of eighteen.

-Joint provision to be made by both parties to provide medical coverage for all the children born to the marriage. The court has granted you, Nora Bell, the legal custody of all six children. Visitation rights have been granted to respondent based on a mutual agreement.

After she stated the terms of the divorce, she gave her blessings and wished me a bright future with my children. I continued to stand before the judge, speechless.

'Was that it?' I wondered.

This was much quicker than the wedding ceremony. I managed to find words to thank the judge then left the court-room with my attorney and Jane. Turning to my attorney I asked, "Am I really divorced? Is there anything that can change this? I just can't believe it was that simple."

Smiling at me with some words of reassurance he replied.
"Yes Nora, it's all over and it is final.
Jane and I exchanged a warm embrace.

"Yes child, you're free at last. Give thanks. Give thanks. Nora everything is going to be alright."

We entered the elevator and headed for the first floor. "Jane, I just want to express my thanks to you for being there for myself and my children. She leaned over took my hand and said, "Nora, I've been put in your life for a reason, and I will always be here for you. What is really important is that after fourteen years of being in bondage, you're finally free."

When she dropped me off she said, "We'll have to take some time and celebrate later."

I leaned over and kissed her on the cheek.
"Thanks again Jane. You've been more than a friend you've been like a mother."

The minute I walked in the door, I called the children together to give them the good news. I noticed Julius was missing, and then remembered he had a meeting with his guidance counselor.

"Finally!"

Everyone yelled and cheered as the kids hugged me.

Soon the phones were ringing non-stop. Most of my family and friends knew the abuse the children and I endured and they were also aware of the challenges I had in getting the divorce. So everyone in my life felt that this was time to celebrate.

When Julius walked in the room I was on a long distance call with my family in Jamaica. The minute I looked on his face I knew something was wrong.

"Excuse me Mom, but we need to talk."
It sounded urgent, so I hung up promising to call back later.
"Congratulations on finally getting the divorce, but we have some other business to attend to."
"Go ahead, I'm listening."

"I just came out of a meeting with my guidance counselor. The good news is, I'll definitely graduate from high school as I ended up with a 2.3 GPA. However, I know you don't want to hear this, but college is out of the question."
I looked at him in disbelief but didn't respond.

"My grades have improved a lot because if you look at my report cards I've moved from failing grades to A's and B's. But because my grades were so low for the first two years it didn't makeup for the last two years even though I was doing really well."

He paused, then continued, "Mom, I've tried, but I get the feeling that I've let you down."

I remained deep in thought for a while before responding.
"Julius you've made significant improvement from D's and F's to almost straight A's in the past two years and I'm very proud of you. It required a serious commitment on your part and you demonstrated that by effecting a positive change. So why can't we implement a plan to get you in college, just like we did for your promotion to 11th grade?"

"Mom, you don't understand, college is different. You're required to have a certain GPA to get in and if you don't, then you just don't get in. The truth is I can work at the car wash full time so I can start making more money. Plus I'll be able to help out with the bills; you know you need the help anyway."

This child's defiance was getting to me, but I tried hard to remain calm. "Julius, I've managed to pay my bills up to this point and not once have I asked you for help. You'll never live long enough to see me budget someone else's money to pay my bills. I can only budget mine. But let me remind you of a few things. If we had accepted the results from your report card two years ago, you'd be a high school drop today. But you know we have certain standards set for this family; graduating from high school and going to college. Julius you met the minimum expectation because you're graduating from high school. Good job! Now the next step is getting you into college. So don't take the advice of your guidance counselor seriously, he's basing his recommendation purely off statistics."

He looked at me as though I was crazy and made it clear that he was not going to comply, "Mom, I know you'd taken the time off from work to accompany me to the minority admissions program to that college in Tampa. Well, you don't have to worry about it, because I'm not going."
Julius hear me out, you don't plan on attending, but you and I will be attending together. Do you understand the difference?"

He was becoming annoyed and rude. "Positive thinking doesn't get people into college."I had to control my annoyance with his behavior and focus on the objective.

"This is not a game Julius; this is about your life. In addition it's crucial for you to set a good example for your siblings. Remember that article, the eldest child set the standard for failure and the other kids followed his example. As the adage goes, it is better to have tried and failed than never to have tried at all."

CHAPTER THIRTY-SEVEN

"Julius wake up, we only have forty minutes to get to the presentation and you're still sleeping."

He didn't budge. Luther came in the room, shaking his brother as he spoke, "Julius, first of all Mommy's only trying to help you. If you stay home and don't go, you'll never get into college. But for the rest of your life, you'd be wondering what would have happened if you'd gone. This might be your only chance, don't go for me or Mommy Julius, but go for yourself man."

He felt like we were ganging up on him, "Leave me alone Luther, you're beginning to sound just like Mom."

While Luther worked on him, I took out his clothes, shoes and socks. By this time he sat up slowly, rubbing his eyes and yawning with no sense of urgency. He was testing me.

"Listen Julius, I'm tired of your games. We're running out of time and we've got to go. I have all your stuff just meet me in the van in three minutes."

He looked up at me without saying a word. I placed his clothes on the back seat, got in the driver's seat, started the engine and was ready to go when I saw Luther leading Julius out to the van.
"Just sit in the back and get dressed."
He didn't respond but followed my instructions.

Luther came over to my window, "Don't worry Mommy, he'll be fine."

Then turning to his brother he said, "Hey J. I believe in you man."

I had no time to lecture this child, but he had something to say, "Mommy, please don't embarrass me, because I know people from my school will be there."

I ignored him but as I pulled into the parking lot I needed to give him a quick reminder.

"Please remember that my only objective is to get you in college and all I'm asking is that you cooperate. Believe me when I say, this is all about you Julius, it's not about me."

He gave me a half smile, "I do."

As we entered the room they were just getting started. The presenter was the assistant director for the minority admissions program. Students with 4.0 GPA and above were awarded full scholarships and those with 3.0 – 4.0 GPA were given priority enrollment. Julius along with two other students in the room did not fit in either category. Shortly after, we found out that the two students had a 2.8 GPA. I knew that made him cringe, because he stood out as having the lowest GPA in the room.

Dr. Wray, the admissions officer singled out Julius.
"Tell me your name, your school and your grade point average."

"My name is Julius Bell, Cooper City High School, 2.3 GPA. His GPA announcement was so low that hardly anyone heard.

"Son, what was that GPA score again?"
Julius seemed stunned and did not reply, so I answered, loud and clear. "2.3 Sir."

"I'm sorry son, but as much as we'd like to, the university requires a 3.0 for admittance. We'll occasionally make an exception depending on the circumstances, but never for a 2.3."

I believe he sensed that he was destroying the kid's moral, so he made a recommendation, "What I would suggest is that you enroll in a community college and work on those grades. Once you meet our requirements we might consider you."

With his head hanging, Julius mumbled.
"I told you we shouldn't have come."

I ignored him and addressed Dr. Wray.

"Excuse me Sir, but may I please give a brief explanation?"

Trying his best to be cordial he replied, "I'm sorry Ma'am, but there are many students here who've met the requirements and they're our priority."

I persisted. "I do understand Sir, but may I please speak with you?"
I think he recognized my determination.
"You'll have a very long wait."
With that he quickly dismissed me and moved to the next student.

It was then that Julius realized that I was there for a purpose and I was not going to be dissuaded by him or the admissions officer. I was prepared to wait for as long as it took for me to present my case. It was 11:45 PM when the last parents and students were dismissed. In the room there were three staff members from the faculty along with Julius and myself. Dr. Wray knew why I waited and was now able to give my son his undivided attention.

"I'm sorry if I came across abrupt earlier, but first I want you to understand that I cannot promise anything,"

Turning to Julius he said, "Tell me son, what do you have to say about your GPA, that's nothing to be proud of."

I looked at Julius warmly and communicated non-verbally.
'You've got an opportunity to make a good impression. Please go for it.'

"Of my mother's six children--."

Dr. Wray interrupted and with a look of disbelief turned to me and said.
"You did say you're this child's mother?"

"Yes Sir, I am."

"I'm sorry, go ahead son."

"Like I was saying, of the six children I've endured the most physical and emotional scars. After my parents separated I started failing and I had to attend summer school to keep up. My Mom made sure that I knew what commitment was all about, and today I understand fully what it means. She didn't realize how bad my grades were slipping because she had to work single-handedly to support the six of us. If I were to be given the opportunity to attend college I know I would succeed. And as the eldest of six, I have to set a good example for the rest of my brothers and sisters. My mom believes in me and even though I'm doing this for myself, I can't let her down."

Dr. Wray was so absorbed by Julius's address, that even after he was through speaking he remained deep in thought. Turning to me he said, "Mrs. Bell, is there something you'd like to say?"

"Dr. Wray, I've told Julius that he cannot change anything about his past, but he has full control of his future. I've tried to create a loving environment free from fear. I've motivated and inspired him and he's made tremendous progress in the last two years. What if we were to have his teachers write letters of recommendation, send his transcripts and I write a letter supporting his performance. Would there be a possibility for him to be admitted?"

"I cannot give you an answer as we speak, but I'll do everything in my power to get him in. It seems however, that you've had a very challenging life Mrs. Bell, but I do admire your commitment to this child. Statistics shows that most of the minorities in colleges are female, sad to say, but most of our black males are behind bars. This child has potential and I will not sit back and watch him go to waste. Just give me sometime to work on this."

The meeting went on for another thirty minutes. It was approximately 1:15 AM when Julius and I walked out of the conference room. The following day Julius faxed all the relevant documents to Dr. Wray.

CHAPTER THIRTY-EIGHT

My pager was beeping non-stop, the house number along with 911 was constantly displayed. I knew it was Tanya because just about every call from her was a 911 call.

'When there's a real emergency at home I'll never know,' I thought. That was the first thing I was going to say to Tanya once I returned her call.

I was in the area where a friend of mine who was also a single mom lived, so I stopped in to use her phone.

"Mom, why did you take so long to call? This is a real emergency. Dr. Wray has been trying to call you. I can do a three way so you can talk to him right now. Mommy it's about Julius."

"Thanks Tanya, let me have the number, I'll go ahead and call him."

Before she gave me the number she wanted to make sure that I'd call her back the minute I hung up from Dr. Wray.

"Okay honey, I promise I will. Let me have the number please."

"Do you have a pen and paper Mommy?"
This kid could talk; she always had something to say. Without realizing, I hung up while she was still talking.

With mixed emotions I dialed the number, "May I speak with Dr. Wray please."

"Mrs. Bell, I've been waiting for your call."

"I'm sorry Dr. Wray. I've had a full day but I just got the message from home.

"Mrs. Bell I know you're busy taking care of those kids, but I have some good news for you." He paused, "Mrs. Bell, start packing, Julius has been accepted at the university. He will be receiving his acceptance letter in a couple of days, along with some other information."

My heart was filled with joy and mine eyes with tears.
"Thank you Dr. Wray. I thank you from the bottom of my heart Sir, and may God bless you. I promise Julius will not let you down."

As I hung up the phone I burst out in tears. My girlfriend and I embraced. Turning to me she said, "Girl you should be proud, that's one less male off the streets. I hope and pray he makes something of his life."

"He will, he will." I said.

I prayed all the way home, 'God you're so good. Thank you for making it possible for Julius to go to college. Thank you for Dr. Wray.'

Then I could not help reflecting on the words of Julius's father when he left. 'These kids will all drop out of school and end up on drugs.' I guess the little loving and nurturing goes a long way. Immediately I dismissed the negative thoughts and focused on the positive things that were unfolding.

Based on the standards that we had set for our family, Julius's acceptance to college was crucial for our advancement, as a family. Because now that he had set the pace, it was an expectation for all the others to follow.

My family, friends and Julius's grandmother assisted in getting everything he needed for college. Once more, I made my list and as the commitments came in, I crossed out the items he needed for school one by one. We had a surprise send-off party for Julius and he got every thing on the list, and then some. The following morning Luther and I drove Julius to Tampa. The first year he maintained a 4.0 GPA. With Julius gone, the Bell family experienced separation for the first time, but he called frequently and came home on every break.

Luther easily assumed Julius's role, his motto being, 'Leadership by example,' He maintained a 4.2 GPA and was the captain of the cross country and track teams. With his commitment and drive he automatically won the respect of his peers and siblings. After working diligently at the car wash, G promoted him to manager and gave him a substantial increase. Luther saved his money, and at sixteen years old we walked into a dealership and he put a sizable deposit on a new truck for his birthday. Only 50% of the note was financed, which made his payments manageable. This child had been goal oriented from an early age and maintained a certain standard for his life.

Being fully cognizant of the financial restrictions that we faced as a family, his goal was to major in business and finance. Luther was a scholar of the 'Academy of Finance,' while in high school, and was selected #1 in the State, in his category. He endorses the saying, 'Time is Money,' and he has taught his siblings the value of time and the importance of money.

Luther, a born again Christian is not a fanatic, but is a firm believer in the power and greatness of God. Often encouraging me to read the bible and pray daily; despite my hectic schedule. This child has brought a certain security to my life that I know will ensure the success of this family one day.

When he graduated from the academy of Finance, he invited me to attend the ceremony. When I arrived, the theater was almost filled, so the only available seat was the second to last row in the back. About 12 of the 150 graduates were awarded scholarships. Each of them wrote a brief essay on why they choose to pursue a career in finance. I had no clue that Luther would be a scholarship recipient. The room was still as the presenter read the following.

'I am the second of my mother's six children; she is a single mom who has made countless sacrifices to provide for her children. My family's financial state has driven me to pursue a career in finance. I aim not only to make a substantial contribution to their lives, but more importantly, teach them the principle of how to make and manage money. It has been often said that, 'It's not what you make, it's what you save,' that matters most.

I am grateful to my mother for teaching me the importance of having a positive outlook and the power of goal setting.

'Mom, thank you for teaching me never to quit and for showing me how to use the obstacles that I encountered as reasons to succeed. I will not let you down. I'll always continue to learn from you, and share with you the wisdom I gain.'

I don't think there was a dry eye in the theater. Luther received a standing ovation and he walked straight to the back where I was sitting to give me a warm embrace. I was crying and so were the ladies to my left and to my right.

His high school graduation was two days away and even though Julius had finals he requested the time to be at his brother's graduation ceremony. Luther was among the first set of graduates, being an honor student. As I watched my son receive his diploma, I cried. Julius comically asked, "How come you didn't cry like that for me Mom?"

With the tears streaming down I replied, "You clown, of course I cried for you. How were you suppose to know when you were on the stage receiving your diploma. If you don't believe me ask your sister."

It was then I realized that Lanora too was crying. She had become very close to Luther, trying to beat his GPA score by the time she graduates. Darrel, Patrick and Tanya were cheering for their brother.

We hurriedly left the ceremony and took Julius to the airport to catch a flight back, as he had exams scheduled for 8:00 o'clock the following morning. Julius understood the bonding we had as a family and there was nothing that would have prevented him from attending his brother's graduation. Though away from home, he still maintained the, 'father image.'

One week later I got Luther packed and ready for college, he did not want a party and he asked me not to make a list. He bought everything he needed and I bought him a computer.

The night before he left he called a meeting with the family.
"I'll be leaving for college tomorrow morning and one of my greatest concerns is leaving Mommy. She understands that I must move on with my life, but are you guys willing to give her the support she needs? You must obey and respect her, not stress her. As a matter of fact the use of that word should be avoided in this house. You guys must read your bible and pray daily because you cannot be too busy for God. Mommy, you and the kids please make an effort to attend church more frequently.

He turned to me, "Mommy, I know you have a burning desire to assist in enhancing the lives of single mothers and their children. That is commendable, but with Julius and me gone, your primary focus should be the continued development of these four children. Eventually, there will be enough time to tell the world your story. But for now, these four kids should be your top priority.
Finally, I must pass down the role of leadership to Lanora. As of tomorrow, you're in charge. Do a good job, it will build character."

We all bowed our heads in prayer and asked Gods' blessings especially on Luther as he prepared to leave home. The following morning we set out early and made a stop in Tampa to pick up Julius. Then we continued to Gainesville. Luther and I were familiar with the journey as we had spent two days on campus during orientation. As we arrived we went to housing and collected his keys and with everyone's help he was unpacked in less than an hour. I wanted to get away, I was sad and I didn't know how to say goodbye to Luther.

I returned to the dorm seeming very cheerful but one look at Julius and Luther revealed the dilemma I was facing. It was hard. I picked up my pocketbook and walked away. The other kids and Julius walked swiftly by. What was it that was so hard in saying goodbye to this child? Maybe it was the respect. Never in my life had he ever uttered an unkind word to me. He always seemed so thankful for everything I'd ever done. Then suddenly, a gentle embrace, "Mommy, I love you very much, and I promise I'll make you proud."

Two hours later we dropped off Julius, though a grown man he was so loving and playful. He hugged and kissed his siblings, "You all better take good care of Mommy, and remember Lanora, you're in charge."

He came over to me and kissing me a dozen times, "Hey Mom, check this out, Luther and I, that's your retirement. It's as good as money in the bank. I guarantee, you'll never be in need of anything."

I returned his embrace, "Julius I love you. I love you very much."

The four kids and I drove off in silence. Everyone was saddened. But Darrel broke the silence, "Mommy, how will you manage when Lenora and I leave for college at the same time?"

Before I had a chance to respond, Patrick replied, "That's easy, Tanya and I will take care of her."

CHAPTER THIRTY-NINE

Right after Luther left, Lenora landed a job at my sister-in-law's restaurant as a waitress, while Darrel took over from Luther at the car wash. Financially things were still very challenging as there was no contact whatsoever with Larry.

I continued working in the weight loss industry. But felt that I was not being treated fairly. I was due for an increase but because I made good commissions my boss did not see completing my review as a top priority. I managed to make ends meet, but never had anything extra. So I still continued baking cakes in order to supplement my income.

The first year Luther was in college, he called to inform me that he was recruited to sell books from May 5th to August 17th. He was stationed in Ohio, so I was disappointed he was not coming home for the summer. Of course, I had a million questions but he readily put my mind at ease when he told me that this was a reputable company, and they'd been doing this for over fifty years. I trusted Luther's judgment and though concerned, I managed to encourage him. He made a call home once per week and it was very brief as every minute was valuable. After ensuring that myself and his siblings were okay, he'd end his call by saying, "Mom I have to do (x amount) of units this week, please pray and ask God to help me make my goal."

The program ended right around my birthday and Luther pushed to get home in time for the celebration. The first year Luther sold books he brought home a paycheck in excess of thirteen thousand dollars. He gave me money to buy some suits for work, paid off the balance on his truck and opened a money market savings account. Everyone was very happy for him. When he came home that Thanksgiving, he wanted to know what plans I had for purchasing a home. I was paying over a thousand dollars for rent and he assured me that I could own a home and practically pay the same in mortgage. The only thing that was standing between me and home ownership was the down payment. I had concerns, Luther had solutions. I had so much love and respect for this child that I was not going to argue with him, so I told him I had no disposable income as I was living from paycheck to paycheck. Therefore, I could not afford to save anything at this time.

"You cannot afford not to save Mom, I don't care if it's only five dollars per paycheck, but you must get in the habit of saving."

"Okay Luther, I promise I'll do something about it. As for the house I don't want you to think I'm not ambitious. Of course I want to own my own home, but realistically it won't happen before Tanya leaves for college."

"Mom, do me a favor, act as though you have the down payment in your hand and go out and look at a few homes. But here are a few things to consider before going out. When you're buying real estate Mom, location is the key. In your case, I suggest you look in the school district; the main reason is that the property value steadily increases and also school is easily accessible. You won't have to worry about transporting the kids they should be able to walk to school. Take your time and look around Mom and see what's out there."

That was food for thought, but I couldn't see that happening anytime soon. Because for us to continue living in the same neighborhood we'd need to come up with at least ten to twelve thousand dollars for down payment, closing costs and insurance.

As we approached the New Year, I thought seriously about a career change because staying in my current job would not allow me to change residence. The year went by quickly and Luther was off for the second time to the book field. I received a call from him two weeks prior to my birthday.

"Mom, what do you want for your birthday this year?"

Jokingly, I replied, "A house."

He remained quiet. I felt uneasy because I was only joking.
"So have you been looking around?" He asked.

"Kind of, sort of."

"Well, at least that's a start. So what are the prices like?" He asked.
When I told him, he cautioned me to look at homes where I could afford to pay

the mortgage. I deliberately changed the subject as I didn't want Luther to believe I was depending on him to help me buy a house.

Two weeks later he drove from Nashville, Tennessee to Pembroke Pines, Florida just in time to make it for my birthday. He was looking dirty, hair grown and sun burnt from being on the road for thirteen weeks, knocking on doors and selling books. But it paid off. Luther's check the second year was $26,000. As dirty as he was I hugged him and told him how proud I was of him.

The following day he told me he had to leave for school that evening but he had some things to do and wanted me to go some place with him. We went to a new development which was only a few minutes from where we lived. There were still a few homes that were being built, so we went to look at the model homes.

Luther and I both liked them, so after leaving the model homes I told him I'm going to start looking for a new job and hopefully by next year I'd be in a better position to become a homeowner. He suggested that we go in and talk to the developer and see what types of programs were available. We were informed that the community was almost sold out and there were only two homes left for sale. He explained that in order for us to secure the house we had to leave a minimum deposit of $5,000. Luther looked on me.

"Do you like it?"
"Yes, I do. But –"

"Mom, just give me a minute."

He reached for his check book and wrote out a check. He handed it to me.
"Happy birthday Mom. Use this as the down payment for the house."

Tears rolled down my cheek as I took the check. It was made payable to the Developer, for $10,000 on the memo line he wrote: 'dwnpymt/mom's b/day.'

The sales person was enthralled. He turned to Luther and asked.
"If you don't mind me asking. How old are you?"

"I'm nineteen." He answered.

"Sir, you're one in a million. I'm really impressed."
I could tell that Luther got a kick out of a fifty year old white man calling him 'Sir.'
Then turning to me he said.

"Ma'am you must be very proud of your son."

"I am,"I humbly replied.

Six months later we moved into our new home with the help of family and friends.

In the spring of that year, I received a call from my girlfriend who had left the weight loss industry to start a career in banking. She urged me to get my resume ready as they were hiring managers for the bank.

"The highest position I've held in a bank is a head teller in New York, but I've held other managerial positions and I'm ready to embrace the training in becoming a bank manager."

Myra was pleased with my response, "I know you can and that's why I'm calling you. You've broken records in the weight loss industry, so take the same discipline to the financial arena, not only will you get a lot of recognition but the compensation is far better.

You'll be in a management training program for 6-9 months, so you'll not have your own branch, until you've successfully completed the training."

"Okay, I'm ready. Where should I send my resume?"

"Here's my fax number, but make sure your resume is results driven and you highlight your achievements. Also start putting your portfolio together. Anyone can pad a resume, but a portfolio never lies. Its primary purpose is to verify the information on your resume in a detailed format. So I hope you've been saving all your awards."

Two day's later I was at the nation's largest consumer bank sitting through a five hour interview. The following morning I was offered the job. Again my kids were very supportive and believed in my ability to succeed. As for my girlfriend I promised her that I would make her proud.

After successfully completing nine months of classroom and on the job training I became a qualified bank manager. The primary reason for my outstanding performance was knowing that my children believed in me and that I had to live up to their expectations daily. By doing that I was able to meet and exceed all the company's goals and provide superior service both to my customers and associates. As a member of the President's Club I was asked what attributed to my success. I shared that I made a commitment to my children that I would succeed and I would never let them down.

Lanora had been one of my greatest motivator's, and sometimes when I get bombarded with the challenges of being in the financial industry she'd call at the right time with a word of encouragement,'Mom if anyone can do it, you can.'

CHAPTER FORTY

Luther was in his final year when Lenora and Darrel were admitted to college. It was also his last year selling books so he made sure to get them in the program before he left. During the four summers that Luther worked tirelessly selling educational books he made a little over $100,000.00. Lenora and Darrel were off to a good start due to Luther's coaching and support. After Luther graduated college and left to pursue a career in the financial industry both Lanora's and Darrel's interest in selling books were not as intense.

Back in Tampa, Julius was busy changing both his major as well as his girlfriends. Julius made it known that he was searching for a wife who reminded him of his mother and he'd continue his search until he found the right one. I tried to tell Julius that his focus should be his studies instead of the girls, but as hard as I tried he constantly expressed a desire to settle down. That concerned me as he still did not have a four year degree.

During the course of a year, Julius brought home four different girls he'd been dating. Then he took a long break before introducing me to #5. She seemed okay, but I felt sorry for her as I felt there might be numbers 6, 7, 8 or even 10. 'If only she knew she was just another number,' I thought.
But I quietly hoped she was not because I liked her, however, I was not going to let Julius know. As nice as Nicole seemed, I'd have preferred my son to finish school before settling down.

Well, by the time Christmas came around Nicole broke the record. Instead of being a 'one time guest' she was on her fourth visit to my house. She brought her parents and her sisters and I realized she was from a reputable family. Her parents loved Julius but I was still adamant on him completing his studies before settling down, as I didn't want him to struggle the way I did. All I wanted was for him to secure a good education before starting a family so he'd be able to maintain a decent lifestyle and not have to work ten different jobs.

After Nicole left with her family that night Julius and I had a talk.
"I don't know what's going through your mind." I said. "But I believe you need to re-prioritize your goals and get back to basics. Think about why you went to college in the first place and how hard it was for you to get in. The promises you made not to let me down. Julius, I want you to be happy but I also want you to be successful. I never want you to have to struggle the way I did, and the surest way to prevent that is for you to get your degree. Julius, I don't care what type of degree you get, just do me a favor and get one."

"Mom, don't be funny. I've been doing philosophy for the past two semesters and I love it."
"Good, well get a philosophy degree then."

"It's a tough one and it's not that easy. I'm going to need some time. But Mom, I've always been able to talk to you, but right now you're not making it easy for me. I'm trying to tell you, I'm in love with Nicole and you're not listening to me. All you're concerned about is me getting a degree."

"You're right about that Julius; she seems like a decent girl so what's the hurry?

"Mom, there's no hurry but I have a desire to settle down with Nicole and eventually start a family. You see Mom after my first year in college I decided that I was going to do the dating thing. Been with a few girls but---"

"Hold it right there Julius. I hope you're using protection. There are more black people dying of AIDS than any other race. And that's scary, so I hope to God you know what you're doing."

"You don't have to worry about me, my playboy days are over. I've been tested and I'm fine. So like I was saying, now that I've met the right one I'm ready to settle down. Being with Nicole leaves no desire to be with anyone else. My heart only beats for her, and I know she's the one. We might not have money but we have this bond that's inseparable. Mom I love Nicole with all my heart and she's mad about me."

"Julius, the only thing your heart should be beating for right now is your degree, nothing else should really matter."

"Mom did you ever think that there are people who will achieve greatness if they could only settle down and start a family, mainly because there's a void in their life?"

"Julius do me a favor and go back to school and get on with the business of your education because if you aspire to start a family, you must be in a position to provide for them. That's the bottom line."

That was December, Julius and Nicole returned to college. On Valentine's day I received a call. "Happy Valentine's day Mom."

"Happy Valentine's day Julius, and tell Nicole I wish her a happy one too."

"You mean, tell my wife?" He said.

"I mean Nicole, your girlfriend, or is there a new one now?"
"Mommy, Nicole and I just got married. And that's what I was calling to tell you."

I hung up the phone and all I could see was the word, 'Termination' written across my son's educational plan. I guess the next call would be to inform me that she was pregnant, hence the reason for the courthouse marriage."

'Dear God this is not what I wanted for my son.' I quietly moaned.

Nicole was not expecting a baby and two months later Nicole's family hosted a beautiful wedding ceremony. Myself and all the children were there and Luther was Julius's best man. Some close friends and family members were invited and with both families there were about one hundred and twenty guests in attendance. Nicole made a stunning bride and ironically some of my friends commented, 'She reminds me of you Nora, she could easily pass for your daughter.'

Once the wedding was over, Julius had a renewed commitment towards his studies; he was in school full time and worked part time. He was burning the candle at both ends, but that fueled his energy and he was motivated to get his degree so he could provide for his family. I knew I was wrong and told Julius I was sorry. But in the midst of everything Nicole became pregnant and gave birth to my first grandchild, Mya.

Right before the holidays Julius graduated with a honors degree in philosophy. With over three thousand graduates, Julius was easily identifiable as he was the only graduate to have a picture of his daughter on the top of his cap. At that time Nicole was pregnant again and I quietly prayed that she would not follow in my footsteps. All I wanted was to shield Julius and Nicole from the hardships I endured.

Little Chris was born in the spring of the following year and both Julius and Nicole agreed that two was enough. Julius informed me that he took the initiative and got a vasectomy. He took control of his family. I got to know Nicole over the years and I wouldn't trade her for anyone, a remarkable young lady who was no longer my daughter-in-law but indeed, my daughter.

As Julius promised, he would not let me down. The most committed father I have seen. Having so much practice with his siblings, parenting for Julius is natural. He feeds, changes, bathe the kids, reads to them and takes them for walks. Parenting for Julius is a shared responsibility between himself and Nicole.

He's involved in every aspect of the kids lives. Julius is totally devoted to Nicole as they've planned their schedule around their kids. Julius completed the coarse work for his PHD in two blistering years and only has to write his dissertation. He currently teaches at the university and his goal of becoming a philosophy professor within two years is one that I would not question. Nicole is back in school pursuing her studies in early childhood education.

Once Julius has completed his studies, one of his dreams is for us to team up as a Mother/Son duo and conduct motivational seminars. Julius's focus will be to motivate men to be committed fathers and I will motivate single mothers to invest in their children and help them to succeed.

Living about four hours from home Julius and I speak at least once per week, but Nicole calls ever so often to have my grand daughter speak with me. The high point of my birthday was when I received a call while at work from Mya singing happy birthday to me. When she was through singing, in her soft, tender baby's voice she said, "I love you grandma."

CHAPTER FORTY-ONE

It was late one Saturday night when I returned from a fully paid company trip sponsored by the bank for all the President's Club Recipients. I had a wonderful time in New Orleans, every minute of the day was packed with fun activities along with arwards and recognition banquets. By the time I had arrived home, I was totally exhausted, only wanting to sleep and re-energize. When I enetered the house there was a weird smell, but I could't figure out what it was. But it was so strong that I started to question Patrick about what had transpired in the house during my absence. I noticed that he had that look of guilt on his face and was avoiding direct eye contact. I knew something was wrong and after much probing I found out that parties were held in my house and only God knows what else went on. I was not getting a good feeling and concluded that the weird aroma must be from marijuana or some other drugs. This was frightening, as a single parent I had pretty much experienced everything but had no prior experience in dealing with drugs of any sort.

Disappointment and fear gripped me but I refused to be crippled with pride and cover this behavior. I was not going to compromise my beliefs and my standards and support any involvement with drugs. All I knew is that I was going to nip this in the bud and not wait around for my son to become a drug addict. I told Patrick in no uncertain terms how I felt about his actions and I reminded him about what my mother had always said to us, "Whatever you do in the dark will always come to light." I needed to find out for myself what was the status with Patrick. A light went off in my head to get his urine tested then I remembered that a friend of mine was a toxicologist. I did what I had to do as a mother to get that on the spot and undiluted, there was a lot of friction and harsh words spoken. But I got it. He became upset and left to go out with his friends.
My heart was broken in a million pieces as I tossed and turned and awaited the break of dawn. I made a call and was at the lab to hand over the sample urine

to get tested, again, another long suspenseful day. I was hoping that all my fears were unfounded and Patrick was drug-free. When I received the call I almost crashed when I heard the toxicologist confirming that Patrick tested positive for drugs.

My crazy side kicked in and I went home and packed everything I could find of Patrick's, he was only sixteen years old but I was not going to allow him to stay under my roof and corrupt Tanya. I packed all his belongings in several black garbage bags and placed them at my front door, then I called the local police department and requested that they come by to escort him out when he arrived home.

The police officers arrived before Patrick and they could not believe the steps that I was taking. They encouraged me to give him a chance as he did not have a record and he was under the legal age of eighteen. They realized after awhile that I had no intentions of changing my mind, so during the debates Patrick walked in. Right there and then I told him that we had to part company as this is not a behavior that I will ever tolerate. I reminded him that I have raised him right and made countless sacrifices and have paved a successful path for him to follow. But since he decided that he wanted to take another route he had to go it alone as I would not support or enable his lifestyle. I told him that he could return home on two conditions as long as he stayed in school and graduste and also for him to be totally drug free, without any evidence of drug in his blood.

The six months that followed was heart wrenching. Many nights I could not sleep as I wondered if Patrick had somewhere to lay his head. I can tell you about tough love because I have truly put it to the test. I learned from Tanya that Patrick was in school everyday but did not speak to her. Somehow I felt that God was working behind the scenes.

One evening late January when I returned from work Patrick's high school diploma was on the dining table with a note attached.

"Mommy, this is for you. Thank you for showing me 'Tough Love' sometimes I thought you didn't love me, but I know you do and I'm going to make you proud, maybe not in your time but I will eventually. My best friend has moved to Tallahassee and now that I've graduated from high school I'm moving in with him. Sorry for all the disappointments I caused, but I promise I will make it up to you one day. Call me when you get home and please come to visit sometime. I love you."

Tears, tears, so many tears that I could not control. Thank God I didn't lose my son and I knew in my heart that he was safe. Patrick attended Tallahassee Community College for approximately two years. One day I received a call from him, "Mom, I'm trying to do things the traditional way, but it's not working. Would you be upset if I dropped out of college and work full time with my company."

"What exactly do you do Patrick?"

"Mom, my company does special events and we have some of the largest parties here in Tallahassee. Clean fun with college kids having a blast. There's a lot money to be made and I could do so much more if I could give it 100% focus."

"As long as you promise that you're going to work and take care of your responsibilities and never ever get involved with drugs again."

"Mom, that was a brief phase of my life. My commitment to never do drugs again is not for you but for me. That was a distructful path and I will not destroy my body or waste my life away. Drugs is a temporary fix and I am interested in some positive long term benefits and I cannot get that by doing drugs. Mom, I promise that you never have to worry about me ever doing drugs again. I now know the effects of making the wrong choices and with the help of God I will do right from now on."

I wiped a tear as I assured him of my love and commitment to support him.

 Back in Gainesville Lanora and Darrel grew very close. For two semesters they shared an apartment, but between Darrel's art and his music production, the place was never quiet enough for Lanora to study. Majoring in child psychology, she does a lot of research in the libraries but many times wanted to come home to study but having Darrel as a roommate did not make it conducive. Lanora maintains an A/B average in college, she's been very consistent with her goal of becoming an elementary school principal. Lanora plans to take a year off after acquiring her first degree to spend some time and dabble in modeling. 'Just for the experience. It's something I've always wanted to do,' she said.

Lanora has the height, all of 5'9" tall, slim with very distinct facial features. However I always felt apprehensive about modeling. I love my daughter so much that I'll always encourage her, feeling confident that she'll eventually do the right thing. After completing her modeling stint, she plans to return to the university to pursue a graduate program to obtain her masters degree, after which time she'll move towards fulfilling her dream of becoming a teacher.

Lanora has a deep admiration for her brothers, because of her love for children she believes Julius is the best father she's encountered and Luther is the most focused and committed individual she's known. Lanora is the motivating arm in our family, always giving compliments and words of encouragement.

One year after Lanora and Darrel returned from the book field I was invited to attend an award ceremony held for the top producers and their parents. The kids were given an opportunity to speak or write about the person who motivated them most. And she wrote a beautiful poem about my impact on her life.

The presentation was very special and as always I could not stop the tears of joy. Darrel and Lanora were awarded for outstanding performance. Darrel was the recipient for the, 'I Wanna Win,' award. The directors of the company invited Luther to present the award to his brother.

Right after the award ceremony it was time for everyone to come together for Christmas holidays. All the children came home and Luther decided that it was his turn to sponsor Christmas. Under the tree, gifts were stacked high. Luther had been dating Crystal for over two years and when they pulled up in the driveway, his Expedition was loaded with gifts. Over forty more gifts were added to what was already there. Luther brought gifts for everyone but most of the gifts under the tree were for Mya and Chris. Mya was Luther's goddaughter and Chirs was Darrel's godson.

I had the pleasure of meeting Crystal before and thought she was a good match for Luther, a gorgeous, professional female who attended university in New York. Luther and Crystal dated for a while before he brought her home to meet me. He'd told me that whoever he brought home would be the woman he'd marry as he didn't have time for the games. So we knew it was only a matter of time before Crystal became a part of the family.

The Christmas celebration was memorable and everyone returned to their respectful homes. It was mid January, a bright and early Saturday morning when my phone rang.

"Hello." I sleepily answered.
"Mommy, its Luther, Crystal and I just got engaged.
"You're kidding."
"No I'm not, I wanted you to be the first one to know."
"Well, congratulations. I'm really happy for you."
"Let me talk to Crystal."
"Congratulations, I wish you guys all the best. So how do you like the ring?" I asked.

"It's everything I've ever dreamed of. I can't wait for you to see it," she said.
"Gosh, you sound really excited, let me talk back to Luther because I want to hear how he pulled it off."
"Yeah, I want him to tell you all about that part."

"Mom I'd been planning this for some time now. The ring was sitting in my safe deposit box in the bank, right during the holidays. I knew in order to do something really special I needed someone to work with me, so I had to get Darrel involved. Remember Darrel's first painting that he doesn't want to part with? Well, I don't think you know this, but Crystal is crazy about it. Plus, it would fit perfect with my décor. When I realize that Darrel wouldn't give me the painting, I offered him $300 and he refused. Anyway I went to the bank yesterday and secretly removed the ring from the vault, so when I came home I told Crystal that I just received a call from Darrel and he'd agreed to give me the painting. She was ecstatic.

'Come on Baby, let's go get it now before he changes his mind.' She pleaded.

'Sweetheart, I had a long day so can we please do it first thing in the morning?'

Well, this morning when we left the house it was still dark. By the time we got to Gainesville the sun was just raising. When I knocked on Darrel's door he came out rubbing his eyes.

'Hey guys. I'm sorry to have to break this to you but I've got a major challenge. You know Lanora went to Nashville for sales training. Well she's scheduled to arrive at Jacksonville Airport at 10:30 AM. My truck is not working man. So can you guys please pick her up for me?'

"Mom you should have heard me, I had to play it off because Darrel and I had this whole thing planned. And Crystal had no clue. So I hollered at Darrel."

'Is this why you brought me up here to pick up Lanora? When are you guys going to stand on your feet and learn to do things on your own? I just get the feeling that I'm being set up and I would definitely have beef with you, if you change your mind about the painting.'

'I'm also a man of my word Luther. Mom raised us right man, so my integrity is as important to me, as yours is to you."

"Mom we argued for a good ten minutes or so, when I felt Crystal tugging me."

'Luther, stop the arguing and come. You don't want your sister to be at the airport waiting with no one there to pick her up.'

"Mom, I was upset the whole way to Jacksonville. So when we got to the airport, Crystal was walking ahead of me and I knew the time had come for me to ask the big question. So I called out to her.

'Hold on Crystal.' She slowed down a bit, but was busy looking around for Lanora.

"I caught up to her, held both her hands and gazed in her eyes."

'First I have a confession to make, then I have a statement and finally I have a question.' I felt as though I was watching a love story as everything seemed so vivid.

'My confession: Lanora is not flying in from Nashville. Lanora is in her bed sleeping in Gainesville as we speak. I brought you here today because three years ago, it was in this very spot that we first kissed.

My statement: I am thankful to God that He's blessed me with such a beautiful woman. Crystal, you have no idea how much I love you.

My question:"Mommy by this time I was on my knees and I slipped the ring from my jacket pocket."

'Crystal, will you marry me.'

"Crystal seemed like she was in a daze. But she positively answered 'Yes,' to my question. I rose from my knees and holding her gently. I kissed her. By this time we had an audience cheering us on. When we finally let go, Crystal looked at her finger and when she realized that it was not a dream she started screaming. . Mom, we are both very happy and I'm thankful to God for everything."

"Congratulations again. So when is the wedding?"

"Not for another two and a half years. My company recently informed me that I'll be in line for a management position by fall of this year. Mom, I want to be financially stable by the time we're ready to have our kids. I want to be able to take time off to be with my kids in their formative years. As I mentioned to you, now that Crystal has her bachelors she'll be doing her graduate studies in South Florida. So by the time we get married, she'll have her masters and I'll be in Senior management in the investment arena. So together we should have a pretty decent income."

In the background I heard Crystal asking Luther about the painting."

"Sweetheart, that was a joke. Darrel would never part with his painting. But let me ask you a question. Which would you prefer, the ring or the painting?"

"Honey forget about the painting, I'll take the ring over the painting any day."

CHAPTER FORTY-TWO

One night as I lay in bed I received a call from Lanora. It was always a pleasure to hear from her because she always had something uplifting to share.

"Hey Mama, how are you doing?"

"I'm doing fine sweetheart. How are you and Darrel doing?"

"We're doing okay. Mom, you were on my mind so I just wanted to call to let you know I love you. Mommy, I was just lying here reflecting on our little family and I'm so thankful for everything God has done for us. Do you feel like talking or are you gone to bed?"

"Lanora, you know I always want to talk to you."

"Ah Mom you're so kind. Anyway, Darrel and I spent last weekend with Julius and Nicole and we had so much fun. They have such a good relationship always catering to each other's needs. Julius treats Nicole like a queen, just the way you've always wanted to be treated. Your grand kids are adorable. Mya is so smart she knows her ABC's, she counts and she knows all the parts of her body. She also knows the animals and the sounds they make. Mommy she's not even two and a half yet and she'll be reading before the end of the year. Chris started to walk and he's saying a few words. But he's going to learn really fast because Mya is teaching him everything she knows.

Mommy, Julius is the best dad I've seen in my entire life. He's right on top of the kids schedule, he matches whatever Nicole does. Parenting to them is a shared responsibility, like it's supposed to be. Believe me Mom, they have a model relationship. While Nicole and I were spending time with the kids, Julius and

Darrel were making beats.

That's really cool Mom, because they're both pursuing their education, but they have this common goal that bonds them, and their beats are off the chain. Mommy have you realized that most of your kids have artistic skills? Julius and Darrel collectively have hundreds of beats plus Julius is working on his first novel. Luther just completed his first book; it's titled 'The Other Way.' The targeted audience is everyone, but the primary focus is college students. It takes them through the steps of how to graduate from college debt free, with good credit and secure a good paying job. Tanya and I have a collection of poems which we hope to publish one day also Tanya told me she already has the outline for her first book and will start writing after she starts college. And you know I'll be starting to write a collection of children's book for which Darrel will do the art work. As for Patrick, he's using his socializing skills to throw the largest paint parties throughout America. He told me they're doing a twenty city tour during the next quarter.

"Wow! "Lenora, you're such a kind person. You only say good things about everyone."

"Hold on Mommy. Have you seen Crystal's ring?"

"No, but I've heard it's fabulous."

"You've got to see it. It's platinum with a big square diamond. Mommy, they don't come any better than Luther. I wish I could find a boyfriend like him. I know that there aren't many guys like that out there, but believe me Crystal is one lucky woman."

"I'm sure she knows that and I truly believe Luther is fortunate too. What I like about her is that she's very professional yet so down to earth and I believe she's 100% committed to Luther. But Lanora, don't worry honey—there's someone out there for you. Just ask God to bring someone special in your life and it will happen when you least expect. Keep praying. But since we're touching on everyone tonight, how's Darrel really doing in school?"

"Mommy, Darrel is a B student and for college that's very good. He takes his studies seriously. Sometimes he'll stay up for hours working on his projects because he'll not stop until the job is done. Then he'll leave for the studio to work on his beats. Mommy, have you taken the time to listen to Darrel's beats? They're the bomb. Believe me, one day this kid is going to blow up. He's so passionate about what he does, that I know it will pay off in the long run. He has a talent show coming up and I think we should all be there to support him, so I'll check on the date and let you know."

"I'll see if I can make it, just give me enough notice. But every now and again Darrel will call me to have me listen to one of his beats. The kid has raw talent and I hope and pray he gets a break one of these days."

"Mommy listen to the lyrics of this song it reminds me of our struggles."

Lanora down loaded the music on the IPOD and had me listen to Darrel's hip-hop version of our struggle.

You gotta understand …most of ya peers…they was birth in this wealth…But not us…ain't how we came up…All the way straight from St.Mary Jamaica…To Kings County Brooklyn …We neva knew no silver spoon or no fork…You probably think we was Muslim…how we ain't consume pork…It was grilled cheese mornings… peanut butter, jelly nights…A poor black single parent…workin'for change…And my pops forfeited quick… early in the game if he knew how bad we struggled… man I'm sure he would have came, right?…Rent due on the 6th.. Pops dipped on the same night…Now that ain't right… but what you gone do… hey, that's just life…From then to now, is like day & night…Bliss is just around the bend, I know it seems… like it ain't in sight…Trust me… I know what your pains like…Just to ensure your voice is heard…you on your knees…prayin' twice…But the Lord Jesus Christ…see He change and saves lives…All the pain you see in life…In an instant…He'll make right. But like the good book said…faith without works is dead…Ya man left you, now you forced to be the head…Of the household…So go and get that bread…For ya family…whether you Tamika, Talia or Tammy…
All single mammies…who be livin'with granny…Thinkin'if I had a couple G's… that would really come in handy…Look…ain't no money gonna fall from the sky…And ain't no job opportunities callin' at night…What you want in life…get up and grab it…I'm fed up and had it…Of seein'families who be set up in attics… Yeah you got government aid…and lunches is paid…But…there's no tomorrow if you don't hustle today.

"So what do you think Mom?"Lenora asked.

I couldn't answer because I was all choked up and tears were streaming down my face.

"Mom."

No answer.

"Are you crying? I hope it's positive tears this time, because there's so much for you to be proud of. Just imagine your first daughter graduating from college in a week and right after your last child leaving for college..."

CHAPTER FORTY-THREE

The Florida sun lit the entire universe as six car loads of us drove up to Gainesville to see Lanora walk. We had built a reputation to have the loudest cheers at graduation ceremonies. Graduation in our family was a major event, bigger than Thanksgiving and believe it or not bigger than Christmas too. Ever heard the saying, "Bigger than life?" Well that's our take on graduation, BIG! It literally opens up a world of endless possibilities.

When Lanora walked we tore the house down. Of course my screams were mixed with tears but even after she returned to her seat I couldn't stop crying. Kevin's warm embrace and encouraging words dried my tears. But not for long because as soon as I hugged Lenora I started crying again.

"So let me ask you Mom, are you going to cry this much when I leave for college next week?"Tanya asked.

"Tanya, I think I'm getting older because of late I cry for everything."

"I don't know about all that but please try and save some tears for me when I leave."

The celebration continued in Tampa, where Kevin's culinary skills represented. The party went on till the wee hours of the morning and despite a few sips of wine I was sober enough to beat the newly college grad in a game of scrabble.

It didn't seem like a week went by. I was out shopping and decorating for Tanya's going away party. Tanya liked excitement so she invited everyone who knew us from 'back in the days' and everyone who we met since we were 'up and coming.' In all we had about seventy five guests.

When Tanya was asked what she needed for college, she replied, "Well, I'll be going shopping the day after the party so Ammmmmm check or cash will be fine. Well her gifts were in excess of $1000.00, so she went shopping alright.

"Mommy it's funny how Tanya needs three cars to transport her stuff to college when Darrel and I left there was still space left in your trunk after we packed our stuff. Must be nice."

Tanya walked in just in time to hear Lanora's remarks.
"Listen Lanora I've worked hard for everything you see here. I worked right through high school and saved nearly all my money. Mommy makes at least four to five deposits a week in my account from my waitress job, so don't let it seem like Mommy is giving me everything."

"Don't even go there Tanya, I don't know what type of hold you have on Mommy but you get whatever you want… Like her car."

"I paid $500.00 for that car…."
"That's a joke Tanya $500.00 for a 1999 Camry and I paid $3000 for a 1994 Altima… Go figure." She paused for a while before she continued.

"The truth is Tanya, I'm not upset at you. You always seem to get whatever you put your mind to and if you go to college with that attitude you'll do very well."

"I'm not leaving my attitude at home, I'm taking it with me Lenora because this is what has kept me ahead of the game."

"You're such a dork. Let's just get the rest of the stuff in the cars and hit the roads."

Everyone was in separate cars but the cell phones kept us connected, it was as though we were together as we talked the entire trip.

After three and a half hours of driving we were finally in Orlando the place reminded me a lot of New York, big city and busy streets. But despite the fast paced lifestyle there were college students who seemed focused and intent on taking on the business at hand. I quietly prayed for God's guidance and protection on my last child as she started life on her own.

Many hugs and kisses were exchanged and I walked away holding back the tears. A sense of pride and accomplishment consumed me as I made my way thru the busy streets to get on the highway.

CHAPTER FORTY-FOUR

Before long my eyes were swollen with tears, but not tears of sadness, nor tears of fear and anxiety of what is yet to come, but tears of joy. I did it! Against the odds, I overcame my struggles and succeeded. All my children, all six—Julius, Luther, Lanora, Darrel, Patrick and finally Tanya left home and went to college.

After years of serving as a handmaid to an ungrateful, abusive husband and forced to satisfy his sexual indiscressions, I fought relentlessly to attain my freedom.
The four hour drive from Orlando went by quickly. I blasted some hallelujah music as I sang praises and glorified the Lord. In record time I pulled up in my driveway. Before exiting, I closed my eyes and thanked God for getting me home safely.

I removed the keys from my pocket book and opened the door. The house was silent. There were no children asking for permission. There was no husband placing demands on my life. For the first time I was by myself and couldn't be happier with the possibilities that God had in store. The past three decades were spent nurturing and molding six precious lives. Thank God I did everything I could, I poured my whole being into these children and with the help of God, I knew that one day, they would pay big dividends.

Dividends of love, kindness, respect, good work ethics and a commitment to paying it forward by helping others. They understood well about not conforming to statistics and to never give up. They had the same opportunity as every child in college and were taught to be the best at their game. They were going to be respectful and responsible parents. But like me, they also had a passion for single mothers and their children.

I took a deep breath, finally turned the page and began a new chapter of my life.

Today:

Dr. Jason Campbell, Ph.D in Philosophy; (USF)
Professor, Nova University. Author and Publisher

Leighton Campbell, Bachelors in Business Administrations (UF)
Marketing Representative, Federated Insurance
Published Author

Leneen Williams, Masters in Elementary Education (UF)
(Currently working on Children's series)

David Campbell, Bachelors of Fine Arts in Graphic Design (UF)
President, Indighost Entertainment

Paul Campbell, CEO, Committee Entertainment Inc (TCC)
Managing Partner, Dayglow Tours & Kreative Catch

Trish-Ann Campbell, (UCF)
Petty Officer, United States Navy
(Ghost-Writer, Editor)

Coming Soon...

Forever Young at 50+
100 Compelling Stories of Love, Survival & Success
By: Nina Hart
To be released summer 2010 (Annual Series)
Submit your stories early for 2011 edition:
submissions@youareyoung.com

Like Daughter, Like Mother ...
Pulmonary Embolism, the Silent Killer
By: Nina Hart
To be released winter 2010

Unstoppable At 30 and Under...
100 Stories of Young Millionaires,
Over-Achievers, Extra Ordinary Talent & Beauty
By: Nina Hart
To Be Released Summer 2011 (Annual Series)
Submit your Stories early for the 2011 edition:
submissions@unstoppableat30.com

The common theme in Ms. Hart's books:
Staying YOUNG, Promise of HOPE, Desire to WIN,
Determined to NEVER GIVE UP...

About The Author:

Nina Hart, God Fearing, Resilient, Driven, Motivational Speaker and Mentor. Her original version of Crosses to Bear, Love to Share was released in 1997, her goal was to inspire single mothers and give them HOPE, and that she did. Nina has appeared on National Television here in the US and Jamaica, has had numerous radio interviews, book signings and also print media. Thousands have been positively impacted by her story. One night Nina received a call about 1:30 AM and while sobbing uncontrollably the caller assured her that she was at the point of committing suicide, but after reading her book she recommitted to her children, "Only death can separate me from my children," she sobbed. Statistics states that 90% of children who witness a parent being abused will become abusers. Well, Nina Hart, mother of six, defied statistics. She was adamant that her sons would not become abusers. She refused to accept that her children were from a broken home, there was nothing broken about their home. Part-time work was a privilege and going to college was not an option. The biggest celebration in their family was college graduation. Her children were raised in a Christian home where the foundation was laid by biblical principles. The new 'Crosses To Bear, Love to Share, transitioned six children to becoming focused and driven individuals, with a burning desire to help change the world. This family is on a mission to make a positive contribution to the Society, and believe me, they are.

If you are a parent needing help with finding grants for your children's college, visit Amazon.com and look up, The Other Way, The Guide To A Financially Successful Graduation, By: Leighton Campbell.

Endorsements

Every parent needs to read this book to see how the Heroine in the story fought to get her eldest son in college with a 2.3 GPA. (Son), "Mom, you don't understand, college is different. You're required to have a certain GPA to get in and if you don't, you just don't get in." Not only did she get him in college, but today he is a Professor, who holds a PhD in Philosophy. In my role as a Philanthropist I come across children everyday who have been neglected by parents who dropped the ball. Thank God she did not, as Society now stands to benefit from six individuals who are committed to changing lives.

Irene Korge, Women's Committee Officer, Big Brothers Big Sisters, Co-Chair Miracle Makers Foundation, Miami Fl

"No matter how many books we read, there will be one...maybe two....that seems to speak words we have spoken before, cried sobs we have wept before, touched nerves we have sensed before in a compellingly familiar way. This book, this journey in words, is one such book. Thank you Ms. Hart. "

Marcia Barry-Smith, Executive Director Bank Atlantic Foundation, Board Member, Women in Distress - Broward County, Florida